CROSS, Peter

Stop smoking

Stop smoking

52 brilliant ideas to kick the habit for good

Peter Cross & Clive Hopwood

brilliantideas

CAREFUL NOW

We hope that you enjoy this book and it gives you lots of ideas and food for thought. We would like to stress that the suggestions we offer ought to be seen as a complement to rather than a replacement for the help and support that you get from your general practitioner. Why not take a copy of this book along to the surgery next time you go, and discuss the ideas with your doctor? We hope you find a way to beat the habit, but we can't be there to stub out the cigarettes every time you experience a moment of weakness – ultimately whether you stop smoking for good is up to you. Good luck!

First published in 2006 by
The Infinite Ideas Company Limited
36 St Giles
Oxford
OX1 3LD
United Kingdom
www.infideas.com

A CIP catalogue record for this book is available from the British Library.

ISBN 1-904902-44-8

Brand and product names are trademarks or registered trademarks of their respective owners.

Designed and typeset by Baseline Arts Ltd, Oxford
Printed by TJ International, Cornwall

Brilliant ideas

Brilliant features

Each chapter of this book is designed to provide you with an inspirational idea that you can read quickly and put into practice straight away.

Throughout you'll find four features that will help you get right to the heart of the idea:

- *Here's an idea for you* Take it on board and give it a go – right here, right now. Get an idea of how well you're doing so far.

- *Try another idea* If this idea looks like a life-changer then there's no time to lose. *Try another idea* will point you straight to a related tip to enhance and expand on the first.

- *Defining ideas* Words of wisdom from masters and mistresses of the art, plus some interesting hangers-on.

- *How did it go?* If at first you do succeed, try to hide your amazement. If, on the other hand, you don't, then this is where you'll find a Q and A that highlights common problems and how to get over them.

Introduction

Smoking killed both our fathers. Hardly a surprise: if you continue to smoke throughout your adult life, as they did, there's a fifty–fifty chance that the grim reaper will take you away with a smoking-related illness or condition. Clive's much loved elder brother dropped dead from an aneurism aged only 55. Two of Peter's siblings continue to smoke, so the chances of losing at least one of them this way are pretty high.

Given the devastation that smoking has had on our lives, it might seem perverse that early chapters of this book rave about smoking. In the short term at least, smokers get a number of benefits from their cigarettes: a buzz that hits the brain seven seconds after inhaling, a sense of belonging to a worldwide club, a shared graveyard humour and a feeling that you are a little more alive than sensible non-smokers. To give this up a smoker needs to subject him or herself to a bereavement process. And to do so includes acknowledging the fun bits of this fatal attraction.

Considering that cigarette advertising has been largely outlawed in many other countries, including the UK, you might wonder why we have included a chapter on it. We do so as adverts from the past linger on years after they have been banned from billboards, cinema screens, magazines and newspapers. Tobacco barons might be evil and cynical, but they are not stupid and know how to package and market their product. They have employed the best designers and advertisers in the business. Nor have we overlooked the glamour that Hollywood gave these lethal little tubes.

Having established what people enjoy from smoking, we move onto the considerable benefits of stopping. Every smoker knows the damage this habit does, but even we were surprised to find how extensive that damage is. You know that cigarettes make your teeth yellow, but are you aware of the damage they do to your gums? You know that smoking adds a few wrinkles to your features, but did you know that recent research has found that a sixty-year-old smoker who has consumed a packet of twenty a day for forty years has the body of someone seven years older than themselves? These and other discoveries add up and are worth considering.

Mostly, however, the book is given over to ideas to help you give up, whether it's joining a support group, using nicotine patches or other drugs, or going cold turkey. We've also included a chapter for someone wishing to help a smoker give up and another on finding that person.

In short, we have adopted and adapted ideas from all over the place. Our thanks in particular go to the dozens of useful and informative websites available on the internet. Just type the word 'Tobacco' into your search engine and behold!

The great thing about the 52 Brilliant Ideas book series is that each chapter comes with a practical task, something that you can actually do. Some, like our suggestion for smashing up your ashtrays, are enormous fun; others, like giving money to a cause you hate if you break a pledge to stop smoking, can be pretty hairy.

There are many books around offering to help you give up, but we believe our publisher's concept is ideally suited to this subject. You will not find here a promise that if you read this book you will quit smoking, nor are we offering a one-method-suits-all approach to giving up. Every smoker is different: what works for Fred Jones in the office may not to work for Samantha Smith in the pub. Indeed, what might not have worked for Fred five years ago may now do the trick. People give up when they are ready and not a moment before. But the process can be nudged along with the suggestions, strategies and solutions you'll find here. What we offer is a huge menu to browse over and from it you can select your own quitting cocktail.

Clive's motivation for writing this book is that he really wants to stop. His daughter desperately wants him to stop. He's read all the books, tried every method you can think of. He's lost count of the number of times he's tried to stop…and failed. So he knows what he's talking about.

This time he's determined it's going to be different.

The method he's chosen is to co-write his own book and read it. With the help of Peter's input as a non-smoker, as well as using a combination of the methods suggested in the book, Clive has used himself as a guinea pig to test out if it works.

This is our first joint writing venture. We thought long and hard about how to co-write this book. In the end, we decided to work out the broad content and divide up the chapters between us. Unsurprisingly, it soon becomes apparent who has written what. Clive, for example, considers he's a smoking addict and often writes in the first person. Peter doesn't and he avoids using terms like 'addict'. The last thing you need is to be hectored by a non-smoker. We feel that smokers will not be offended by the way one of their own describes himself. But the ideas and views you'll find in this book are shared by us both and represent our thoughts on the subject.

We would like to take this opportunity to acknowledge the support of numerous friends to whom we spoke during our research, and in particular the support and input from our wives, Sabina Dosani and Pauline Bennett.

The fact that our fathers smoked was central to Clive's decision to start and Peter's decision not to. And so we remained until we sat down to write this book: someone who couldn't give up and someone who hadn't been able to start. It would make a great conclusion to assert that in writing our roles have been reversed – that Peter had taken his first cigarette and Clive had smoked his last – but life, like quitting smoking, is never going to be that neat.

Writing this book has been a journey for Clive. All stories, a famous writer once said, have a beginning, a muddle and an end. And every story needs an active question: in this case, if this book is any good, by the time it's finished Clive will have stopped smoking. And Peter will be even more determined not to begin. Turn to page 234 to find out how it ends.

1

No smoke without fire

Please feel free to smoke while you read this book.

The pleasures of smoking — let us count the ways. If it wasn't such fun to smoke, nobody would do it. We need to celebrate why smoking lights up our lives.

Let's face it, we're addicts. For one reason or another, we made the fatal decision to start smoking. We smoked that first cigarette and it was all downhill from there. And now we can't stop.

Oh yes we can.

SMOKING IS COOL, BUT NOT AS COOL AS IT WAS

Fifty years ago three out of four men smoked. Today it's just one in four, about the same as for women. So either a lot of people died young or lots of people quit (actually it's a bit of both). Choose which you'd rather be – dead or an ex-smoker.

There are over 12 million ex-smokers in the UK, and if they can do it, so can we. More than 1,000 people a day stop smoking in this country. You could be one of them. My friend Ann, who's a writer, said to me, 'To stop me smoking you'd have to take me to the top of a tall building and throw me off.'

Here's an idea for you...

Write a list of all the reasons why you want to give up smoking. Photocopy it and pin it up in every room in the house and at work, so that you're constantly reminded.

Tempting, but there are less drastic ways, and this book explores them.

We've all heard the scary stories about smoking and its effects. It's okay to be scared because, despite what the tobacco companies tell you, they're mostly true. Now I'm not trying to terrify you – you know most of this stuff anyway – but, just to remind ourselves what it's about before we launch into all the different ways we can give up, let's celebrate the cigarette.

PLAYTIME

Smoking is relaxing. Smoking helps you concentrate. Smoking keeps you awake. It also picks you up when you're down, it calms you when you're stressed and it finishes off a job well done, a good meal, the day, lovemaking. It's everything to all people. No substance on Earth can do all these things at once, surely? And yet most smokers will say that's exactly what this wonder drug does.

Take the pleasure of that first cigarette of the day. Hard to beat. Or any cigarette after a long period without one. (Sadly, that's what any addict will say, whether their drug's heroin, crack cocaine or even coffee.)

The warm glow of a cigarette in the dark, the curling plumes of smoke as they drift skyward. All this plus the rewarding hit as the nicotine flows into your bloodstream and presses the deep satisfaction button.

But there's more to enjoying cigarettes than just the chemical hit – in fact, there's a whole raft of other pleasures.

HAVE YOU GOT A LIGHT, BOY?

Cigarettes, their packets and a glittering array of fashion accessories make smoking a designer's paradise. There's the smooth, clean-lined cylinder of the cigarette which fits so well it could have been designed to slip between your fingers (it was). Then there's the smart, glossy design of the packets, with their clear colours and sharp lines. They fit so neatly into the pocket or the handbag, it's a joy to hold them.

On top of that, there's the allure of the lighters, holders and cases. Ashtrays can be works of ceramic excellence, or reminders of some favourite distant place or football team, conjuring up the good things in our life.

Lighters are an art form in their own right. From the cheap and cheerful throwaways to the glamour of a really classy one or the iconic Zippo, your lighter not only lights your cigarettes, it says something about you as a person as well.

Take a long look at all the poisons you're filling your body with when you smoke in IDEA 10, *What's your poison?*

Try another idea...

'It has always been my rule never to smoke when asleep, and never to refrain when awake.'
MARK TWAIN

Defining idea...

'[Cigarettes are] not legitimate articles of commerce, being wholly noxious and deleterious to health. Their use is always harmful.'
Tennessee Supreme Court (upholding a total ban on cigarettes, 1898)

Defining idea...

3

CELEBRATIONS, FIREWORKS

So, as you prepare to stop, relish those last few days of smoking. Really look for all the pleasures it brings you – at the same time as listing all the negatives that come with it.

Smoking is truly the complete experience. Pity it kills you at the same time. It's like saying goodbye to an old friend who's trying to murder you and won't stop until he succeeds. Who needs friends like that? Time to stop.

How did it go?

Q   I've been smoking for over 30 years so it's a bit late to stop now, isn't it?

A   *It's never too late to stop. You can add years to your life and make sure that your later years are not spent in agony. Question yourself honestly and see if you are just fooling yourself into thinking that you wouldn't be better off (in lots of ways) as a non-smoker.*

Q   I really enjoy smoking. We're all going to die anyway, so where's the harm?

A   *You have to ask yourself whether you enjoy living. If the answer is yes, then you should look at the other things you like doing and carefully question how many of these you will able to do if you contract lung disease, have a stroke or fall foul of the many other life-threatening conditions that smoking leads to. What will your quality of life be like then, and is it worth the risk to carry on smoking? It's like cutting off your nose to spite your face – and that might just happen if you carry on smoking!*

Turn right off Tobacco Road

Belonging to a tribe is an important human desire. Other smokers are just the same as us and revel in their status as social pariahs.

There's comfort in numbers, especially in times like these, when smokers are made to feel like latter-day lepers. Here are some suggestions to help you become a lapsed smoker without alienating your former chums.

Smokers and non-smokers are members of different tribes. This doesn't mean that they don't talk, relate, work or even marry outside the clan, just that they belong to different tribes. There are a few – a very few – people who only smoke at parties or have one cigarette or cigar at Christmas, but these people are as common as transsexuals so don't really count. Clan members recognise their own and the other side. Smokers can identify an abstainer as easily as if the words 'sensible non-smoker' is tattooed on their forehead. Perhaps this is why non-smokers are never offered a cigarette. Smokers recognise someone who is wavering and needs to be pulled back on board with a gentle 'go on, have one of mine'.

Of course people do smoke in private, but there is a huge social component to the habit. Smokers bond, huddle together and do so increasingly as their numbers

Here's an idea for you... **Stand outside your workplace with your smoking colleagues and see if you can last a tea break without lighting up. Find your own way of telling everyone you are there for their company, the gossip or the craic. If you're really struggling, you can always say you're not smoking for a bet.**

decrease and attacks grow from passive smoking victims, do-gooders who know what is best for you and, worst of all, reformed ex-smokers: the born-again breed hunting for would-be converts.

It seems to us that one difficulty in giving up is the sense that one is letting the side down, changing camps and moving in with the enemy. Instead of being a member of that cosy collection of people who congregate outside the office for a smoke at tea breaks and the end of lunch you will be joining the smug disapprovers inside. You might be worried that once you give up you'll be barred forever from the casual chat and endearing intimacy that fellow puffers share. You could, of course, stand outside the office with them, but will you feel happy and relaxed watching them smoking and will they be comfortable with someone who refuses a light?

SAY NO BUT STAY IN WITH THE IN CROWD

You can learn a lot from our mate Derek, a fifty-a-day man, who worked his way up from a furtive drag behind the school bike sheds to hard-core member. OK, he had moved from Player's No. 6 to Silk Cut, but he was never one to go on about giving up or even cutting down. One day he stopped. 'I'm giving up for my little girl,' he said. 'It was her birthday last week and I asked her what she wanted.' Then it all tumbled out, the whole story: how he'd asked her what she wanted, bracing himself in case she used it as a chance to get a pony or something else out of his price range. But she didn't; she looked him straight in the eye and said she wanted him to quit smoking. She was eight, had never complained before about his habit and out it came, 'Give up Dad, for me'. He was so gob-smacked that he agreed at once. Only later did he feel cornered and wondered whether Lynn, his wife, had put his girl up to it. But a promise is a promise. And no one is prepared to make him break a promise he made to his little girl.

OLD ALBERT'S DEATHBED

Another variant on this scam is a wheeze we call Old Albert's deathbed. In short, you spin a yarn about visiting an ageing uncle in hospital in the final stages of emphysema. He uses breath from his diminished lungs to tell you how much he regrets his sixty years of high-tar cigarettes before squeezing your hand and saying 'do me a favour, say you'll stop'. You were too choked to say anything to him then, but threw away your almost full pack of Benson & Hedges when you heard he'd died a couple of hours later.

Having a really good reason to give up is a great way of staying in with the in crowd. You could use assertiveness techniques and just say no, but this way is more fun. But beware that you

Ever considered trying to quit while away from the glare from family and friends? Take a look at IDEA 44, *Trial separation*, for our suggestions on how to do it.

Try another idea...

'*I used to smoke two packs a day and I just hate being a nonsmoker...but I will never consider myself a nonsmoker because I always find smokers the most interesting people at the table.*'
MICHELLE PFEIFFER

Defining idea...

'*They threaten me with lung cancer, and still I smoke and smoke. If they'd only threaten me with hard work, I might stop.*'
MIGNON MCLAUGHLIN, *The Second Neurotic's Notebook*

Defining idea...

can lose mates if you keep banging on about how wonderful everything now tastes and how much fitter you feel. There is a real danger that ex-smokers can reek of something far worse than stale tobacco fumes: smugness. And, rightly, they become despised by both camps. You've given up, great. Others haven't, tough. The one thing that all your smoking mates will need to be told is that it's your habit you're rejecting, not them.

How did it go?

Q It's all very well suggesting that I just tell my mates I'm giving up. I've told them so often that every time I mention it now they just smirk and roll their eyes in a 'here we go again' kind of way. What do you suggest?

A   *You're right – if you've told them that you are giving up more than once, why should they believe that this time will be any different? Sometimes people brag about how they are giving up in a way that gets up others' noses. Take a leaf out the Alcoholics Anonymous book and say that you are trying to give up a day at a time, or even trying to get through the morning without one. And bear in mind, proving doubters wrong is one hell of a motivator.*

Q My trouble is that I always smoke when I have a beer. I don't want to stop going to the pub, but for me smoking and drinking are linked. Can you think of a way to stop smoking and carry on drinking?

A   *Indeed they are for a lot of people. Many pubs don't let you smoke at the bar, so if you position yourself there you'll have a good excuse not to light up.*

3
A question of taste

What kind of smoker are you? Having some idea of the scale of your problem will help you form a plan of action to beat it. Answer this simple questionnaire to create a profile of you as a smoker.

And be honest.

1. How many cigarettes do you smoke a day?

2. How much does smoking cost you per year?

3. When was your first cigarette?

4. What was it that made you smoke that first cigarette?

5. When did you first realise that you were addicted?

6. When did you first decide to give up?

7. How many times have you tried to give up?

8. When was the most successful time and why?

9. Why do you think you relapsed on other occasions?

Here's an idea for you... **Remember those charity thermometers which showed the rising amount of cash raised? Work out roughly how much you spend on cigarettes per week. Now colour in your own thermometer week by week and see how much you've sent up in smoke.**

10. Why do you want to give up now?

11. Has anybody else urged you to stop and why?

12. How will you or those close to you benefit from your stopping?

13. What would you do with the money you save?

14. How much do you think your health will improve having stopped?

15. What health problems do you have now that you think might be caused by smoking?

16. Do you smoke in your home?

17. Are you alienated sometimes because you are a smoker?

18. Do you avoid public transport, especially long flights or train journeys, because it is non-smoking?

19. Do you get up in the middle of the night for a cigarette?

20. You're an intelligent person (you must be – you've bought these Brilliant Ideas). What one thing do you think is most likely to convince you to stop?

YOUR SMOKER'S PROFILE

Having identified some of the factors that make up you the smoker, see if you can identify yourself from the thumbnail profiles below, then check to see what to do next.

Look at the nature of your smoking habit in IDEA 23, *First of the day*.

Try another idea...

The social smoker

You only smoke at parties, Christmas, New Year and Give Up Smoking Day (because you're a free spirit and a rebel). You're dicing with death, so don't tempt yourself – the Tobacco Demon's waiting to pounce and get you into his evil clutches. Next time you feel dangerous and want a cigarette, pause for thought before lighting up, then think again.

The casual smoker

Smokers find you baffling. So do non-smokers. You smoke once in a while (usually someone else's). Why bother? Why play Russian Roulette with a deadly drug? Be good to your body and set a good example to your smoker friends. Quit now while you're ahead. If you ever want to smoke another cigarette after reading this, don't.

The dope smoker

Talking of heads, it's still more or less illegal to smoke dope in a lot of countries, Holland being a notable exception. Chances are that if you started smoking dope by you'll now be hooked

Check out the poisons you're putting into your body every time you smoke by reading IDEA 10, *What's your poison?*

Try another idea...

on a harder drug – the nicotine in cigarettes. Not that we condone breaking the law, but if you have to smoke dope take up a pipe (you can buy some really neat ones in Amsterdam) or bhong (a water pipe). Just stop cigarettes – they're bad for

'Tobacco is a dirty weed. I like it.
It satisfies no normal need. I like it.
It makes you thin, it makes you lean,
It takes the hair right off your bean.
It's the worst darn stuff I've ever seen.
I like it.'
GRAHAM LEE HEMMINGER, *Tobacco*

your health. If you find that you can wait until tomorrow to find your dealer but you're desperate for a cigarette, think twice.

The serious smoker

You smoke upwards of 20 a day. Other people's image of you is usually with a cigarette in your hand or dangling from your mouth. There's always time for just one more cigarette. Before you go out. Last thing at night. Before you eat. After you eat. Even between courses if you're dedicated enough. You urgently need to give up. And if you've never tried, it's not as hard as you might think and the benefits are enormous.

The lapsed smoker

You've lost count of the number of times you've tried to give up and failed. Don't despair, it's a tricky habit to kick. Think of your previous attempts as merely rehearsals for the big one – the time you put all your resources into the final push to kick the weed. Never give up giving up. Now's as good a time as any for that successful attempt. Try again.

Q **I only smoke now and then. I can stop any time. So what's the problem?**

A *Okay. Why wait? Do it now. Dare you.*

Q **I've smoked all my life. Surely it's too late to stop now?**

A *It's never too late to stop, and you'll feel the benefits almost immediately. It could add years to your life.*

Q **I really enjoy smoking; indeed, it's one of my main pleasures in life. Why should I stop?**

A *It's your choice, of course, but ask yourself why you've invested in these Brilliant Ideas in the first place. There must have been the twinkling of an interest somewhere to motivate worth. There could well be something hidden in these pages that rings a bell. But if nothing strikes a chord, fine, carry on smoking. See in five years when the penny drops. Smoking kills and it's going to kill YOU.*

How did it go?

Curse Sir Walter Raleigh

It's history lesson time. Cue good-looking intellectual waltzing around in front of televisual landscapes (use your imagination). Let's track back through the mists (hazy smoke?) of time and find out how it all started.

If we're wise, we learn from the past. And we've centuries of the mistakes, lies and downright stupidity of our smoking ancestors to learn from. The smoke signals have been there for ages — can you read them and change your future?

The Huron Indians believe that long ago the Great Spirit sent down a woman to provide the people of the Earth with sustenance. Where her right hand touched, the soil grew potatoes, where her left hand touched, corn. When the Earth had been made fertile she sat down to rest. Beneath where she sat grew tobacco.

Tobacco originated in the Americas around 6,000 BC. Its uses by the American Indians included smoking, chewing and hallucinogenic enemas. Strangely, the last of those doesn't seem have caught on in the same way as smoking.

Here's an idea for you... **Check out www.tobacco.org/ resources/misc/losses.html to see the impressive death list Walt and his friends have contributed to over the years.**

CERTAIN DRIED LEAVES

On Columbus's journey to the New World in 1492 he received 'certain dried leaves' as gifts 'much prized' by the native Arawak tribe. He threw them away. Rodrigo Jerez discovered tobacco smoking in Cuba and took the habit back to Spain. However, the plumes of smoke frightened his neighbours and he was imprisoned by the Holy Inquisition for seven years.

But the root had taken, and on his release Jerez found that the Spanish had gone crazy for the weed. Over the next century tobacco was introduced into France, Portugal, Spain, Turkey and Poland, and spread along trade routes of the world by sailors. It's thought that Sir John Hawkins and his crew first introduced tobacco to England around 1564.

Doctors in Europe began to claim tobacco as a wonder drug, able to cure dozens of illnesses, including hysteria, worms, falling fingernails and cancer. (Got that one wrong then, eh guys?)

WHERE'S WALLY?

So where, you ask, is Sir Walter Raleigh? Enter the biggest Wally of them all. Taught to smoke by Sir Francis Drake, then given a long-stemmed pipe invented by Ralph Lane, the first governor of Virginia, he became a convert and turned on Queen Elizabeth I. He smelled money.

Thanks for buying one of our books! If you'd like to be placed on our mailing list to receive more information on forthcoming releases in the **52 Brilliant Ideas** series just send an e-mail to *info@infideas.com* with your name and address or simply fill in the details below and pop this card in the post. No postage is needed. We promise we won't do silly things like bombard you with lots of junk mail, nor would we even consider letting third parties look at your details. Ever.

Name:...

Address:...

....

e-mail:...

Which book did you purchase?...

....

Tell us what you thought of this book and our series; check out the 'Brilliant Communication' bit on the other side of this card.

I am interested in the following subjects:

☐ Health & relationships
☐ Lifestyle & leisure
☐ Arts, literature and music

☐ Careers, finance & personal development
☐ Sports, hobbies & games
☐ Actually, I'd be quite interested in:...

And just to say thanks, every month we'll pick 3 random names from a hat (ok, it may be some other cylindrical device) and send a complimentary book from the series. It could be you. So please tell us what book you'd like:..(check out www.52brilliantideas.com for a full list of our titles, or if you prefer we can choose one for you based on your subject interest).

You can change your life with brilliant ideas.

We're passionate about the effect our books have and we have designed them so that they can become an inspiring part of your daily routine. Our books help people to grow, giving them the confidence to believe in themselves and to transform their lives. Every day, around the world, people are regaining control of their lives with our brilliant ideas.

infinite ideas

www.52brilliantideas.com

BY AIR MAIL
par avion
Royal Mail

IBRS/CCRI NUMBER:
PHQ-D/9423/OX

NE PAS AFFRANCHIR

NO STAMP REQUIRED

RESPONSE PAYEE
GRANDE-BRETAGNE

Infinite Ideas Ltd
36 St Giles
OXFORD
GREAT BRITAIN
OX1 3LD

Brilliant Communication

- If you enjoyed this book and find yourself cuddling it at night, please tell us. If you think this book isn't fit to use as kindling, please let us know. We value your thoughts and need your honest feedback. We know if we listen to you we'll get it right. Why not send us an e-mail at *listeners@infideas.com*.

- Do you have a brilliant idea of your own that our author has missed? E-mail us at *yourauthor missedatrick@infideas.com* and if it makes it into print in a future edition or appears on our web site we'll send you four books of your choice OR the cash equivalent. You'll be fully credited (if you want) so that everyone knows you've had a brilliant idea.

- Finally, if you've enjoyed one of our books why not become an **Infinite Ideas Ambassador**. Simply e-mail ten of your friends enlightening them about the virtues of the **52 Brilliant Ideas** series and dishing out our web address: www.52brilliantideas.com. Make sure you copy us in at *ambassador@infideas.com*. We promise we won't contact them unless they contact us, but we'll send you a free book of your choice for every ten friends you email. Help spread the word!

The author of *Worke of Chimney Sweepers* (1602) concludes that tobacco might have the same effect as soot. It dries up man's 'unctuous and radical moistures' – proven by how effective it was in helping to cure discharge in gonorrhoea. But in the long run it could also dry up 'spermatical humidity'. The author concludes that tobacco must damage memory, imagination and understanding.

People began to identify the fact that tobacco smoking was an addiction around 300 years ago. But the deadly poison nicotine is only half the answer. Find out more in IDEA 20, *Smoke screen*.

Try another idea...

King James I wasn't as impressed as his predecessor and in 1604 published his famous *Counterblaste to Tobacco*, describing it as a noxious weed and slapping an import tax on it. Thus big business and government for the first time combine to make serious money out of tobacco.

OFF WITH HIS HEAD!

Sir Francis Bacon noted in 1610 the increasing use of tobacco and observed that it was a hard habit to quit. China banned tobacco in 1612, followed by Russia in 1613. By 1614 there were 7,000 shops in London selling tobacco. King James made the import of tobacco a royal monopoly – you had to pay the king £14K a year for the privilege.

In 1617 you faced the death penalty in Mongolia for using tobacco (now there's an idea). In 1620 Japan banned tobacco. In Turkey in 1633 up to 18 people a day were executed for smoking. In 1634 Czar Alexis of Russia ordered whipping, a slit nose and transportation to Siberia for a first offence, execution for a second offence (no one offended a third time). In 1638 China beheading was the punishment.

'Curse Sir Walter Raleigh, he was such a stupid get.'
JOHN LENNON

Meanwhile, England, France, Spain and Italy went for the big bucks to grow and market American tobacco. During the Great Plague of 1665–6 smoking was made compulsory at Eton to ward off infection.

SLAVES TO THE WEED

Growing demand meant that the state of Virginia legalised lifelong slavery to create the manpower to work the developing tobacco plantations. George Washington used his 300 slaves for just this purpose.

When Captain James Cook arrived on a Pacific island smoking a pipe the natives threw water over him to put him out (now there's another great idea!).

Tobacco crops served as collateral to fund the American War of Independence.

Throughout the seventeenth century doctors were discovering some of the downsides of tobacco, linking it to cancers of the scrotum, nose and lips. Lung cancer at this time was very rare.

By 1828 nicotine has been isolated from tobacco smoke in its pure form. It was considered a 'dangerous poison'.

A Turkish soldier is credited with inventing the cigarette at the Siege of Acra in 1832, using paper tubes in which to wrap the tobacco, in the same way as they had rolled gunpowder for their cannon.

The mid-nineteenth century saw the creation of most of the major tobacco companies, from Philip Morris in London to Gallaher's in Ireland, and Washington Duke in the USA (later to become British American Tobacco Company). By 1884 Duke's company was producing 744 million cigarettes a year.

'Never let the bastard back in my room again – unless I need him.'
SAMUEL GOLDWYN

Defining idea...

ONLY TWO THINGS ARE CERTAIN IN LIFE: TAXES AND DEATH

By 1900, 4.4 billion cigarettes were being smoked worldwide every year. By 1911 Duke's American Tobacco Company controlled 92% of the world's tobacco business. By 1950 America alone produced 327 billion cigarettes a year. Nowadays, a single cigarette machine can produce over 8 million every day.

Despite growing medical evidence of the dangers of smoking, governments (taxes), big business (profits) and smokers (addiction) are so in love with tobacco that the industry has continued to grow like a cancer.

Millions have died unnecessarily from the effects of smoking. Let's make sure we don't become just another fatal statistic.

Q   Why do I need to know all this stuff?

A   *You don't. Kind of interesting though, isn't it? Always struck me that Walter
'I don't have the head for smoking' Raleigh introduced a sort of Trojan
Horse to the world. All in the name of profit. The whole history, like that of
most addictive drugs, is one of greed.*

**Q   How come all the attempts to ban smoking have failed, even with
the threat of death?**

A   *Ask the tobacco companies and the government: there's just too much
money at stake. Oh, and by the way, it's not a threat of death, it's a near
certainty. Smoking kills.*

5

The seven stages of man giving up

Other smokers have given up before you and experts have plotted the phases most of them go through.

For most of us, stopping smoking is a slow and difficult road. Knowing the route, where you are, helps you get to your final destination quicker.

Giving up isn't easy. The road to recovery is paved with people and setbacks determined to get you puffing again. It's been calculated that the average smoker needs four or five false starts before he or she finally weeds out the weed from their life and becomes an established ex-smoker. A depressing thought, until you consider that most successful activities are built on a foundation of apparent failures. Toddlers run and fall before they walk. It's only through the process of falling down that they learn they have to slow down: that they need to stand and balance before they can move forward without toppling over – and take one step at a time.

Professor James Prochaska, a leading health psychologist, and his colleague Dr Carlo DiClemente have identified seven stages on the road to giving up, with a contented smoker who isn't thinking about quitting at one end through to someone who has given up but is having the occasional relapse at stage seven. The difficulties arising at each stage are different, so help needs to be tailored accordingly.

Here's an idea for you...

Plot your own road to giving up smoking in seven stages. Think up your own quitter's milestones to show your progress – the more colourful and detailed the better. Where are you now? What will you need to do to get to the next stage and the one beyond? And how will you stay there?

...and another idea...

If you are contented to continue smoking we challenge you to get on the internet and have a look at the lung pictures on http://www.presmark.com/ htmlfile/

Stage one: pre-contemplation

People at this stage have no intention of giving up. Why should they? As far as they're concerned the advantages of smoking outweigh the disadvantages. Take Tim. At dinner parties he jokes that at his place it's the non-smokers who are kicked out onto the lawn and get talked about by the smokers. This always gets a huge laugh: everyone knows that Tim hasn't got a lawn. According to Prochashka and DiClemente, people like Tim are denying the negative effects of smoking and can only see the advantages.

Stage two: contemplation

During this phase you are increasingly aware of the risks involved in smoking but are not prepared to do anything about it. However, people who have got this far are likely to try to give up within the next six months. Only half the smokers who reach this stage succeed in giving up for more than a day. But people at stage two are becoming increasingly aware of their reliance and the effect it is having on them, and may have explored alternative ways of quitting.

Stage three: preparation

At this stage the smoker wants to quit, seeing smoking as a problem that needs addressing. They may be taking active steps, like setting a quit date and thinking about support structures to help them.

Stage four: action

Good intent is replaced by an attempt to stop smoking. This phase continues until not smoking starts to feel normal, which could last anything from one to six months. During this stage you may need help coping with nicotine withdrawal and suggestions to help you adjust to a non-smoking lifestyle.

Another way of looking at and dealing with the quitting and relapse cycle is described in **IDEA 24, *Smokes and ladders.***

Try another idea...

Stage five: maintenance

When you have got to this level your life starts to feel comfortable without cigarettes. You have started to master cravings and the times between these urges grow wider.

'The cigarette does the smoking – you're just the sucker.'
Anon.

Defining idea...

Stage six: termination

By now you are no longer hooked on smokes. You are conscious of what precipitates the need for a cigarette and can cope with these feelings. But Prochashka and DiClemente warn that, even years after stopping, 90% of ex-smokers are tempted to have a puff and may return to their old level of smoking.

Stage seven: relapse

Setbacks, warn Prochashka and DiClemente, are a natural part of quitting. However far you get, once you start smoking you go back to stage two and will have to start all over again.

'The best way to stop smoking is to just stop – no ifs, ands or butts.'
EDITH ZITTLER

Defining idea...

23

How it helps

Knowing what stage you are at gives you a reasonable insight about your chances of giving up. At stage one you are unlikely to give up, but things could change if you started to realise the downsides of smoking: cost, cough, smelly clothes as well as the big C.

How did it go?

Q **I find it difficult to know where to put myself on this sort of scale. When I'm out with friends and we are all smoking I haven't got any worries and giving up is the last thing on my mind, yet when I'm alone and think about it – especially the health implications – I'm desperate to give up. How can scales like this one help me?**

A *These are just broad groupings and most people are unlikely to be stuck in one zone all the time. In essence, scales like these are designed as a tool for professionals, a rough guide when they are attempting to assess someone's attitude and dependence. While it sounds like you are might be at stage one when you're with friends, the reflection you are doing suggests that you might be further on than you think.*

Q **Putting smokers in little boxes according to how addicted they are is all very well, but how can it help me?**

A *A good question. The short answer is that many smokers are a lot more addicted to cigarettes than they realise. Scales like these are based on getting hard evidence from tough questions. You are only likely to quit smoking if you have some insight into the grip the habit has on you.*

6

Imagine

Create a picture in your mind's eye that puts you off smoking.

It may need a bit of practice — even riding a bike can feel weird at first — but once you've got the hang of it, it will feel second nature and something you'll never forget.

One quality that marks humans out from other animals is the ability to imagine. Without it, nothing could be built. Saint Paul's had to exist in Christopher Wren's head before hundreds of workmen converted his drawings into a cathedral, and the same is true of cars, aeroplanes, great paintings – and crap ones – and works of literature. Most of us haven't got the imagination of Wren, the Wright brothers or Wagner, but we can use our imagination to see things that are not there and make mental images of things that are hard to get our heads around.

We all know the dangers that smoking poses, but do they motivate us to stop or even cut down? Larger and larger health warnings on the sides of cigarette packets could just as well be written in a foreign language for all the impact they're likely to have; likewise, graphs showing the increased likelihood of contracting lethal diseases barely register on our collective psyches.

Here's an idea for you...

Think up your own smoking-related nightmare scenarios: the more morbid the better. Write them down or draw them and keep them with your packet of twenty. If you are stuck for ideas, get suggestions from friends and family.

On the other hand, if you are able to convert the risks into pictures, you will convert indifference into feelings and become motivated into actually doing something. Here are a number of ideas we have come up with. See if they resonate with you.

Shrouds

As you look into a packet of cigarettes try to visualise them as people who have died of lung cancer wrapped in paper shrouds and packed into mass graves. You could theme these groups: the golden age of Hollywood, musicians, royalty, people I know or have worked with, and so on.

Bullet

Imagine each cigarette as containing a lethal bullet that may or may not explode. As you place each of these loaded missiles into your mouth, imagine it's a loaded gun you're putting there. If it helps, think of the climax in the *Shawshank Redemption*, when the governor reached into his office drawer, removed a pocket gun then blew his brains out.

Cremation

Next time you light up a cigarette, cigar or pipe with a match or a lighter, pause to look at the flame. Now imagine a huge flame burning up your body in a crematorium because you have died prematurely from a smoking-related illness. Imagine this every time you light up.

Stamping on butts

When you see someone grinding a cigarette butt into the ground imagine a jackboot coming down on a human face and smashing out the remains of life. Each butt representing one more nail in your coffin.

Poisonous cloud

You're in a club or pub where most of the punters are smoking. The air is thick with smoke. Imagine the environment is full of carcinogenic agents (it is!) or, better still, blue asbestos that is keen to make a beeline for your lungs.

Tar tar sauce

Next time you chance across a gang of workmen resurfacing a road, check out their huge container of tar: a thick, jet black liquid. Imagine that stuff dripping down your throat and coating your lungs. It might takes years or decades, but each drop of this dark glue is reducing your lungs' capacity to do their stuff, providing the rest of your body with life-giving oxygen.

Coughing chorus

Smoker's coughs are acquired over time. The one you have now may be no great shakes, but amplify it and imagine yourself choking on your own vomit, drowning in your own fluids.

Feel like using your imagination in a positive way? IDEA 48, Don't give up giving up, can give you some pointers.

Try another idea...

'People always come up to me and say that my smoking is bothering them...well it's killing me.'
WENDY LIEBMAN, American comedienne

Defining idea...

'So smoking is the perfect way to commit suicide without actually dying. I smoke because it's bad, it's really simple.'
DAMIEN HIRST

Defining idea...

Sad old man or woman in the corner

When you're out and about it won't be too long before you come across a lifelong smoker on their last legs, fighting for breath as though someone has placed a plastic bag over their head. See the way they smoke: relief, not pleasure; an attempt to stay calm, not cool. Imagine that's you a couple of decades hence.

How did it go?

Q   Isn't all this stomach-churning stuff a bit over the top?

A   *Sadly, no. Smoking may be a legal habit that is still socially acceptable (though maybe not* de rigueur, *as it was a few decades ago), but the harsh facts are that one in two smokers will die of a smoking-related disease. Some have described it as a slow form of suicide, but one in two odds is a pretty poor bet.*

Q   I'm sick of people trying to make me feel guilty about smoking. It's my body, so why shouldn't I be free to use it as I feel?

A   *We'd be the first to agree. But we would contest that smokers have been subjected to a whole raft of brainwashing from tobacco barons and other forces. Making up your own images of what is actually happening to you can help you fight back. These are only our suggestions – we haven't made them to make you feel guilty but to give you a few ideas to get your creative juices flowing.*

7

Fat is a former smoker's issue

One advantage of smoking tobacco is that you are putting something in your mouth that won't be translated into a higher reading next time you step on the scales.

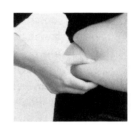

Some, though not all, smokers gain weight after giving up, so what can be done to prevent this happening?

Cigarettes have fewer calories than celery and that's saying something, as the effort taken to chew this most boring of vegetables uses more energy than it contains. Understandably, then, many smokers worry that giving up means certain weight gain. They fear a cycle of disempowerment, loss of confidence and loss of self-respect. You may have already given up, hated your new, fuller figure and reverted to smoking to regain your former shape. You'll hardly need us to tell you how demoralising it was and how it puts the dampeners on further attempts. So what was going on?

Food tastes better

Smoking dulls your taste buds, effectively smothering your meals and snacks with a blanket of nicotine. Quit smoking and your taste buds are reawakened. It's the gustatory equivalent of switching from an old black and white television to digital colour. No wonder you'll want to eat more.

Here's an idea for you...

Explore a whole range of fruits, from grapes to strawberries, melons to cherries, sultanas to bananas. Go further and check out raw carrots, celery, sunflower seeds etc. Select your favourites and use these as nibbles when you feel the need to smoke.

Eating gives you something to do

At times of heightened agitation we can't stay still. Withdrawing from any substance makes you agitated. While nicotine levels in your bloodstream diminish, your body screams for a replacement chemical. And when that craving isn't met you'll start to feel jumpy. Reaching for your packet, playing with matches, lighting the little tubes, puffing and, of course, taking the thing in and out your mouth helps to burn off this surplus agitation. But when you're trying to give up you don't want to reach for that cigarette packet, and the ensuing conflict between your body's desire for more nicotine and your mental resolve is likely to make you even more agitated.

Defining idea...

'During the day I would substitute nicotine for food and during the evening I would food for nicotine. Once you give up, you take control of your life, not only in your eating habits but in all other ways.'
ALLEN CARR, stop-smoking guru

Smoking as a diet aid

Former champion jockey Lester Piggott is said to have smoked cigars to suppress his appetite. Doubtless this did the trick, and he is surely not alone. But taking tobacco for this purpose uses the same sort of warped logic as using amphetamines – speed – or even heroin to give you that chic shape that fashion magazines adore.

Snack attack during smoking breaks

Some research has suggested that non-smokers often eat snacks when their puffing partners are outside having a quick one. And this research also suggests that new abstainers switch over and eat more between meals, replacing one vice with another. You could also throw in those times when you leave a main meal early, skipping an extra helping of apple pie and ice cream, as lighting up in the garden is more tempting.

If weight is not an issue for you, why not check out IDEA 13, *Live fast, die young*, for information on what impact cigarettes have on your health.

Try another idea...

Comfort eating rides to the rescue

For many of us, a very effective way of shutting down this conflict between body and mind is scoffing snacks. Unwrapping a candy bar and savouring it often apes the physical movements of smoking and provides your body with a sugar rush that helps it ignore the nicotine depletion. Trouble is, comfort eating only lasts as long as you chomp, and soon after your last mouthful the cravings return. Isn't life cruel?

Breaking the cycle

Being able to understand what is happening helps you prepare yourself. Nervous agitation can be burnt off with aerobic exercise, like walking, swimming or cycling. In fact, exercise helps in more ways than one. Two or three bouts of serious exercise a week revs up your metabolism and releases endorphins, your body's natural uplifting, feel-good chemicals. In fact, when you exercise, your brain produces a concoction of chemicals that can help you kick the habit. Many of these effects are down to a chemical found in chocolate. It's called phenylethylamine and hits the same brain circuit as amphetamine, causing the so-called runner's high. Exercise also nukes a stress substance called cortisol, chilling you out. And if that's not enough, exercise gives us warm feelings of accomplishment, cranking up self-esteem. So what? Self-esteem is

'I would rather be overweight and not smoking than underweight and dead.'
Panellist speaking to Joel Spitzer

Defining idea...

31

instrumental in stopping smoking. Getting fit, toning up, losing weight and becoming a sexy beast should help you feel a bit better about quitting. If you haven't been doing any exercise for a while, you may even find that in the process of not lighting up you actually lose weight!

How did it go?

Q   **Every time I've tried to give up smoking I've put on weight. It really gets me down and even when I start smoking again the weight stays on. At this rate I'll end up twenty stone. Wouldn't I be better off cutting my losses and give up giving up?**

A   *In a word, no. The health risks of smoking outweigh everything else. People can put on weight for the reasons we've just described. If you can, find an interesting way of exercising while you are giving up. It doesn't have to be organised sport or circuit training, and it might even help you lose weight. Get a dog that takes you for regular brisk walks, buy a bike or take up line dancing.*

Q   **I've found myself buying loads of sweet junk food since I stopped. The weight isn't going on yet, mercifully, but is there something I could do before it does?**

A   *There are low-fat alternatives, but you need to be careful: some still contain quite a few calories. And the good news is that they taste almost as good as the ones that pile on the pounds.*

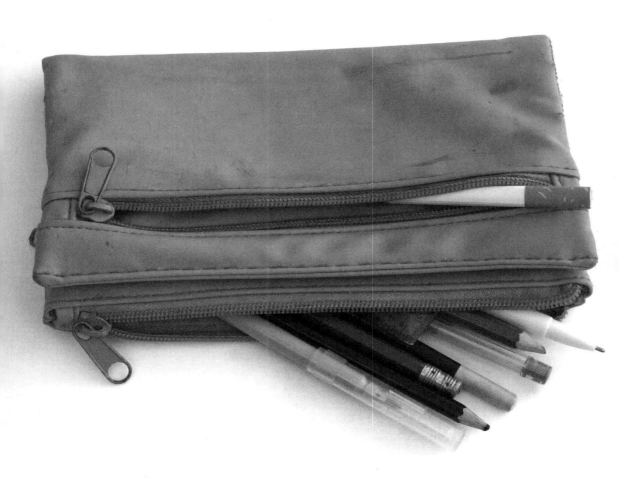

8

Superkings?

Peer pressure when we're young can lead to a (short) life sentence of smoking. What makes us kids think that smoking makes us look older, more good-looking and more likely to get inside somebody's pants?

Ask anyone who smokes whether, if they had their time over again, they'd choose to smoke that very first cigarette and the answer is almost invariably an emphatic NO! So how come so many of us fall into the deadly trap?

Growing up is a challenge. There are all those raging hormones, the striving for independence and the rebellion against adult authority. It's not surprising that we often head for the taboo areas, like sex, alcohol and drugs. It's a badge we can wear to say we're not kids any more.

SMOKE GETS IN YOUR EYES

There are risks, of course, and we're kind of vaguely aware of them or want to be daring. But then when we're young that's what we do – we take risks as a way of

Here's an idea for you...

Talk to yourself. Improvise with a partner or write a dialogue between two versions of yourself – the Smoker and the Ex-Smoker. As an ex-addict, the latter will know all the scams, evasions and lies the Smoker will come up with to not give up just yet. And know how to counter them.

life, because we see ourselves as adventurous. We take risks with no thought of the consequences, no long-term vision of the future, because all there is is today.

But that's all an illusion. It's an illusion that tobacco companies, while they might say they don't take advantage of it, know all too well. They've worked wonders to create a sexy, cool image of the smoker. They create the desire in us to be just like that, like the man or the woman in the image. Trouble is it's an advertiser's con. No question that you can be cool and sexy; what they don't mention is that you don't actually need the cigarette to achieve it.

BE A SPORT

The worse thing about cigarettes is that the danger is well hidden, not least by the tobacco companies. When I was younger I played lots of sports. One guy in my school rugby team, Dave, was brilliant. He was fast and nimble, he could dance round the opposition and be off like a bullet. And he smoked.

I'd been told that smoking was bad for me and all that. So I nodded wisely and waited for Dave to break down, become a coughing wreck and wheeze his way to a standstill. He didn't. By the time I grew up and lost touch with him he was still the fastest thing on two legs.

It wasn't till I met him recently at a school reunion, over three decades later, that the long-term effects became apparent. He still looked pretty fit, but he'd lost all his hair because he was undergoing a course of chemotherapy for his lung cancer and was actually as weak as a kitten. The bullet was spent. Even I could have beaten him at the 100 metres.

CHOOSE A DIFFERENT PATH

Smoking doesn't make you grown up, it makes you a slave, it makes you ill. Maybe not today, maybe not tomorrow, but for the rest of your life. Say no, not because I say so, not because of what any adult says. Say no because you say so. Because you've read some of these Ideas, gone onto the internet and done some research, because you've asked every grown-up smoker you know whether they would choose to start smoking if they were 10 or 15 or 20 again.

SAY NO BECAUSE YOU KNOW BETTER

Take up sports, find a hobby, indulge in self-abuse – anything except start smoking. And if you're a grown-up smoker don't give up warning young smokers whatever they say back to you. Don't just tell them not to, tell them why from your own personal experience. Cough all over them, if it helps.

Even one less new smoker on the planet is better than staying silent, or offering them a cigarette.

Take a look at the older smoker talking to his younger self to prevent him from starting in the first place in IDEA 40, *Older and wiser.*

Try another idea...

'The boy who smokes cigarettes need not be anxious about his future, he has none.'
DAVID STARR JORDAN, first president of Stanford University

Defining idea...

'During the first half of 1981, our research shows that we exhibited far more growth among young adult smokers (eighteen to twenty-four years old) than any other company we plan to pursue this growth with all possible vigor.'
R.J. REYNOLDS, *Global Presence*

Defining idea...

37

How did it go?

Q **Everyone in my group of friends smokes and drinks. It's part of the culture. If I don't do the same I won't be one of the crowd, will I?**

A *Be an individual, make your own mind up and don't just follow the herd. It's not clever or sexy or grown up to smoke, it's just plain stupid. If all your mates put their hands in the fire, would you? Why? Most people don't smoke – so there's loads of other potential friends out there. Perhaps some of your friends are only smoking to be 'in' and are waiting to follow your lead.*

Q **My mum and dad and brother all smoke. They seem to enjoy it. I just want to try to see what I'm missing. Where's the harm?**

A *That's understandable, we all want to explore the big wide world of grown ups when we're young. But you must have twigged by now that grown ups can do some pretty stupid things and not everything they do is worth copying. If you decide to experiment, do this: buy a packet of 20 and, whether you want to or not, smoke all 20 one after another. If you enjoy it carry on, if not don't ever touch cigarettes again.*

9

Smoking gun

The ill effects of smoking take a while to become apparent. They sneak up on us. By the time we notice, the habit has given us cunning ways of ignoring them or making excuses. Hasn't it?

We all slow down as we get older. Smoking, however, is likely to bring you to a standstill. Like the early Daleks, you'll be buggered when it comes to stairs, and you'll have to set off for everything three hours earlier because you'll be living life in slow motion.

Look out for the tell-tale signs. This is a handy guide to the smoke signals, the key things to watch out for which tell you your days may be numbered. Of course, to begin with it'll be small things, things that you feel you can cope with because they don't really seem to be doing you any major harm.

Here's an idea for you... **Boycott the conmen. Refuse to watch or participate in any sport or cultural event which is sponsored by a tobacco company. Write and tell organisers and tobacco companies why you object – start smoking again immediately if any of them write back and tell you: (a) you're right and they'll never do it again, or (b) it's a really cheap way of advertising their life-threatening products.**

TAKE MY BREATH AWAY

Say goodbye to those long, lingering French kisses. No more intimate moments where you whisper sweet nothings in your loved one's ear. Smoker's breath smells. Some smells are okay, this one's a turn-off. Smoking was once seen as cool. No longer.

Smoke smells. Smells linger. Smoke smells linger longer. Clothes, hair, furnishings, cars are all neon signs that say, 'We smoke and we stink but we don't care!' Oddly enough, this is not an attractive prospect to non-smokers, so it cuts down your choice of partners by around 75%.

SMOKE AND MIRRORS

Who is the fairest of them all? (Smokers need not apply.) Take a good long look at yourself day by day and count the lines on your face as your habit turns you into a prematurely wrinkled prune. Your hair grows thin and loses its bounce and lustre. Your fingers yellow, along with your teeth. All classic signs of a smoker.

In the meantime, your bank balance will be showing signs of strain as your habit builds up and you begin smoking more and more. Not to mention the higher premiums you'll have to pay for insurance (they expect you to die younger, you see).

YOU DON'T KNOW WHAT YOU'VE GOT TILL YOU LOSE IT

Your health, that is. Your heart, lungs, oesophagus (and voice), legs etc. And without these, your life. Now you do know, because we'll tell you just exactly what bits of you will stop working, wear out early or fall off if you carry on smoking.

Airwaves

Breathing is a brilliant idea. Everybody does it. Your lungs really like it and so does the rest of your body. Strangling yourself is cheaper and a swifter, less painful, option than smoking.

An early sign is the well-known smoker's cough. This rapidly becomes a morning ritual, whereby you spend a considerable amount of time coughing up as much accumulated rubbish from your airways as the body can expel. Then there's the cough you seem unable to shake off all winter long. The dry cough is caused by the heat scorching your lungs and air passages. This can sometimes be uncontrollable, taking several minutes to clear.

As time goes on, it's the breathlessness that hits. The stairs become a mountain, hills are an Everest and you can't run for more than a few yards. Any physical activity leaves you short of breath and your chest hurts if you exert yourself too much.

Even if you're (comparatively) old and immobile, you can still enjoy the good life with your food. Check out IDEA 38, *This dog's got teeth.*

Try another idea...

'HIV and tobacco are the only two major causes of death that are increasing substantially throughout the world.'
RICHARD PETO, epidemiologist and statistician

Defining idea...

Defining idea...

'Just what the doctor ordered.'
Advertising slogan from Liggett

Heartbeat

Coronary heart disease is nicotine's biggest gift to you. Money may make the world go round, but, more importantly, your heart makes your blood go round. No heart, no you. Don't smoke: have a heart.

Damage your lungs and you damage your heart. As your smoking cuts down the amount of oxygen absorbed into the blood, so the heart has to work all the harder to pump the necessary amount of oxygen to keep the muscles and vital organs going.

The longer you smoke, the more clogged up the lungs become, the harder the heart has to work. Chest pains are a worrying sign and ought to be a serious warning to you that the heart just can't take it anymore.

The problems you'll be causing your blood vessels can lead to a stroke, which can kill you or leave you partially disabled or unable to speak. Classic signs are double vision, terrible headaches or difficulty finding the right words.

Circulation problems can lead to amputation, particularly of toes, feet and legs. Your teeth may also start to loosen if your smoking causes bone disease and your gums recede.

The only real answer is to stop now. At the very least, have regular medical check ups and go and see your doctor immediately if anything worries you. Don't give yourself a death sentence.

Q **I'm nearly 30 and still play for my local football team every week. I only smoke moderately, so why should I worry?**

A *Because the worst effects of smoking only take effect slowly. Give it another ten years the way that you're going and you'll wish you'd stopped earlier. The longer you smoke the more serious the damage, even if you smoke a small number of cigarettes every day. Don't delay, stop today.*

Q **Recently I've found that I'm very short of breath and I get chest pains, but I'm too scared to go the doctor as she might tell me that I have lung cancer or something. Should I just wait and see if it passes?**

A *No! The possibility of a serious outcome is all the more reason to go to the doctor immediately. First, it may be not that bad, and the doctor can put you in touch with the local smoking cessation group, who'll support you while you stop. If it is something more serious, the earlier you catch it the better your chances are of finding effective treatment. Not knowing is more worrying than knowing the worst, believe me. So drop everything and make an appointment tomorrow.*

How did it go?

43

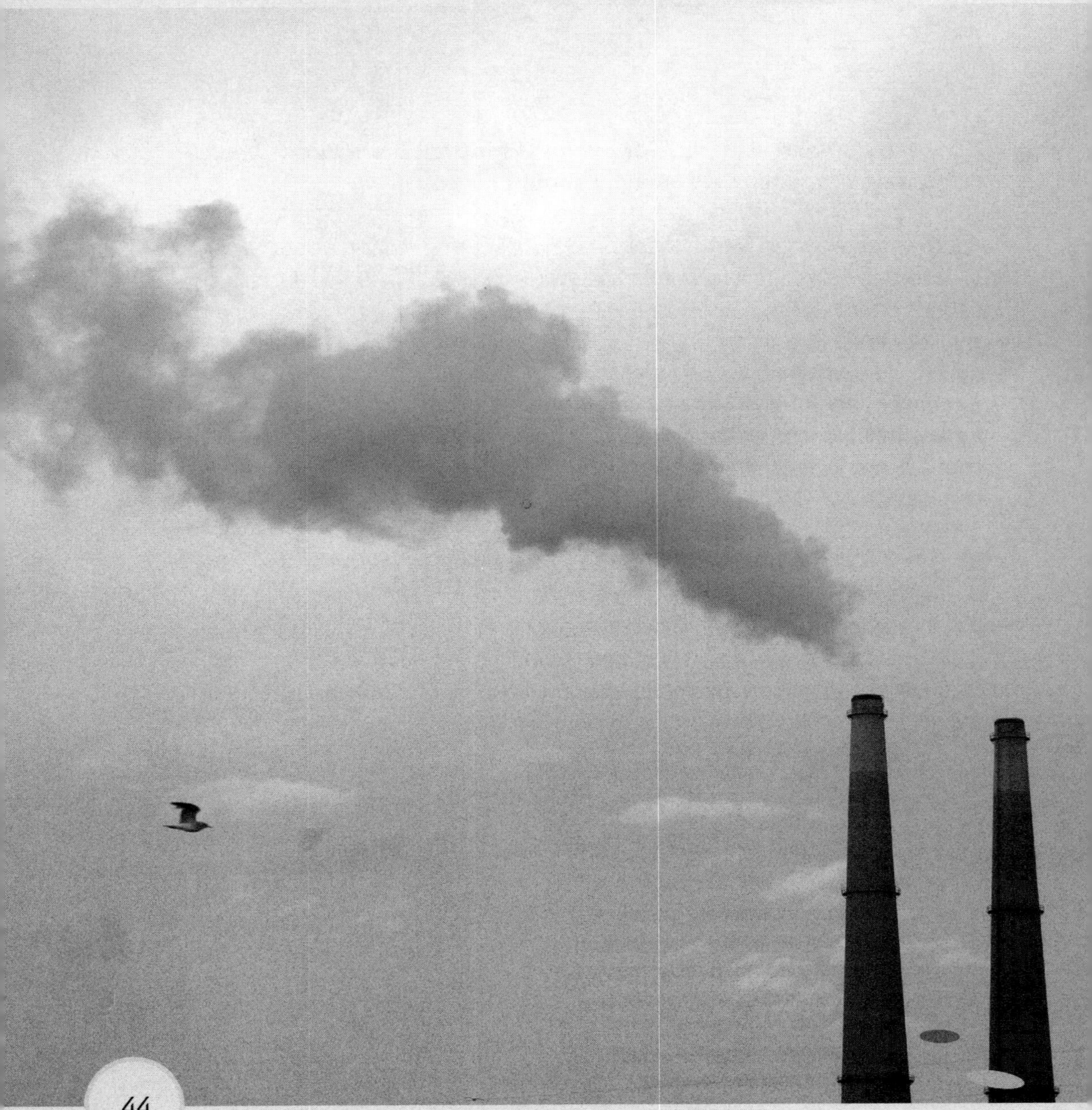

10

What's your poison?

A cigarette contains over 400 toxic chemicals. Line up for your deadly dose of poisons and see just what goes inside your body every time you light up.

Question: What do nylon, embalming fluid, paint stripper, weed killer, mirrors and plastic all have in common?

Answer: They all use ingredients that you smoke in your cigarette.

Lots of people love the thrill of drinking cocktails – the exotic blend of ingredients, the colour and sparkle of the end product when it's brought to your table. You can choose from a menu showing exactly what's going into the drink and gain some idea of what it will taste like.

On a more mundane level, when we go to the supermarket we can pick up a packet or a bottle and read what's gone into a product before we buy. We can avoid monosodium glutamate or saturated fats, aspartame sweetener or peanuts.

Here's an idea for you...
Write a list of what is bad about smoking. Photocopy it and pin it up in every room in the house and at work, so that you're constantly reminded.

How come when we buy our packet of cigarettes all we know is that we're buying tobacco, with a warning that SMOKING KILLS? No list of ingredients to be seen. So what is in a cigarette? Most of us can roll out the three most obvious

Nicotine is a substance found naturally in the tobacco plant. It is, however, also a deadly poison. It takes only seven seconds from inhaling for nicotine to be absorbed into your bloodstream and reach your brain. That's twice as efficient as injecting it into your arm. Nicotine is also highly addictive – more addictive, in fact, than heroin.

Tar is produced as a result of the manufacturing process of cigarettes. You ingest this directly into your lungs when you smoke and it builds up a coating on the alveoli (mini-branches within the lungs) that reduces your ability to absorb life-giving oxygen.

Carbon monoxide is what comes out of car exhausts and your cigarette. In high concentrations it's highly toxic – suicide by cigarettes just takes longer. Carbon monoxide binds avidly to haemoglobin (in red blood cells) in your bloodstream, thereby preventing the uptake of oxygen. Smokers generally have 10–15% less oxygen in their bloodstream than non-smokers. You need the oxygen to power your muscles, so the heart has to pump extra harder to provide it.

These are the main players, but cigarettes give you a whole more!

LET'S HEAR IT FOR CANCER

Cigarettes deliver a positive cornucopia of cancer-inducing chemicals (carcinogens), including the following.

Check out IDEA 7, *Fat is a former smoker's issue*, and see what great things you can put inside you instead of becoming a walking chemical works.

Try another idea...

Benzene causes dizziness and light-headedness, irritates the nose and throat, and may cause an upset stomach and vomiting. It's used as a solvent for gums, fats, waxes and resins, in the manufacture of drugs and the production of nylon, as well as being found in petrol.

Formaldehyde is a highly flammable liquid/gas, used as a disinfectant, germicide, fungicide and embalming fluid, and in home insulation and pressed wood products. It irritates the eyes, nose and throat, and can cause skin and lung allergy.

Selenium increases the risk of lung cancer if consumed in large quantities through smoking. In modest amounts (in nutritional supplements, for example) it's an essential micromineral and an antioxidant. Cigarettes are not a nutritional supplement.

Beryllium causes severe bronchitis or pneumonia after high exposure, and can permanently scar the lungs and other body organs. It's used widely in manufacturing electrical components, chemicals, ceramics and X-ray tubes.

Cadmium can cause malformations in a foetus and reproductive damage, as well as permanent kidney damage, emphysema, anaemia and loss of the sense of smell.

'Some ingredients may be added to tobacco during manufacture for various reasons. It is our policy to assess the appropriateness and acceptability of all ingredients prior to use.'
Imperial Tobacco website, 2005

Nickel may damage the developing foetus, as well as causing coughing, shortness of breath and fluid in the lungs. It is used in electroplating and in making coins, batteries, catalysts and metal alloys such as stainless steel.

[Not to mention polycyclic hydrocarbons, nitrosamines, beta-naphthylamine and 4-aminobiphenil.]

Okay, so now you've set up the ideal conditions for a cancer to start growing (take your pick – lung, mouth, throat, larynx, bladder, cervix etc.). What you need now are some chemicals to help it on its way. Guess what? Cigarettes provide these too. And while we're there, let's throw in a few other toxins for good measure.

ALSO STARRING

Ammonia, used in making fertilisers, plastics, dyes and textiles, is produced by rotting and decomposing animal and vegetable matter. It can irritate the lungs, causing coughing and/or shortness of breath, and can lead to a fatal build-up of fluid in the lungs (pulmonary oedema).

Acetone is an ingredient in most paint strippers and varnish removers. It can make you dizzy and light-headed, and can irritate your eyes, nose and throat.

Hydrogen cyanide is extremely poisonous and can irritate the skin, causing a rash.

Arsenic is a poison often used in insecticides and weed killers (and Victorian murders). Very handy for making some military poison gases.

Lead can cause tiredness, mood changes, headaches, stomach problems and insomnia, and increases the risk of high blood pressure.

Mercury is used in thermometers, barometers, vapour lamps, mirror coating, and in making chemicals and electrical equipment. It's highly corrosive.

[Not to mention cresol, phenol, acrolein (from the burning paper), nitric oxide and nitrogen dioxide.]

'R.J. Reynolds does not – and will not – use any cigarette ingredient if scientific evaluations indicate that it will increase the inherent toxicity of tobacco smoke.'
R.J. Reynolds Industries website, 2005

Defining idea...

Q **If cigarettes have all this rubbish in them, how come they don't taste foul?**

A *Tobacco manufacturers add ingredients like sugar, liquorice, chocolate, herbs and spices to improve the taste.*

Q **You're kidding. You're just trying to scare me. How can something so dangerous still be legal?**

A *Good question. If someone tried to introduce cigarettes onto the market today they'd be thrown out on their ear. Too many powerful interests are involved, that's why. Big multinationals, governments and lots and lots of profit. Believe me, everything written above is true. If anyone tells you different, they either work for a tobacco company, own shares in one or are a politician.*

11

The shock of the old

Growing older is part of life. Smoking gets you there quicker than if you don't.

Not wanting to quit to protect your lungs or heart? Seeing the impact smoking has on your face and body should give you the needed push.

Smoking kills. Every smoker knows that smoking kills. Indeed, dicing with death, when the real prospect of dying seems a lifetime away, is part of the initial thrill of smoking. It gives the habit its edge and glamour, and makes those who smoke feel that little bit more alive and interesting than the sensible types who don't.

Smoking also ages its consumers. A recent research paper in *The Lancet*, one of the world's foremost medical journals, found that someone smoking a packet of twenty cigarettes a day for forty years had at sixty the body of a non-smoker aged sixty-seven and a half. Scientific evidence that deep down even the most hardened and unapologetic smoker knows to be true. The evidence of the ageing effect of smoking is everywhere, even staring out of the chap you shave in the morning or the woman to whose face you apply lipstick.

Talk to a selection of children and teenagers who don't know anything about you (if you dare). Ask them to tell you how old you are – the first number that occurs to them, not a figure to flatter you. You may be shocked to discover that this group think you're older than you are. Adults are more likely to tell you what they think you want to hear.

The question then becomes how you can convert insights like these into motivation providing the impetus to help you quit. The good news is that by quitting now you can move out of the ageing fast lane already congested with other smokers and back in the middle lane, and start rubbing shoulders with those smug, healthy sons of bitches who know how to say no.

COMPARE AND CONTRAST

You might have seen those magazine articles that look at the effect a healthy lifestyle has on individuals. Often what is most striking is the illustrations which compare fit and unfit couples. By early middle age there is already a striking difference. The fit couple weigh less, and have better posture, skin, muscle tone and stamina. They look younger than the artist's impression of the other couple. If you think this is pushing the bounds of reality, take a look at a non-smoking sibling and ask yourself seriously whether they are wearing better than you are.

DOCTORING PHOTOGRAPHS

You're an only child or all your siblings smoke. No worries: doctor, a photo please. Take a recent snap of your head and shoulders, enlarge it and then trace over. On your traced sketch add additional wrinkles around the eyes, forehead, mouth and so on. Add or extend a double chin, thin out the hair. What should emerge is an image of yourself in years to come. While there is no way yet of reversing this process, its speed can be checked by quitting cigarettes.

You are likely to get an even more painful image of your future using a computer software tool like Photoshop. It's widely available, so if you don't have the program, there are sure to be plenty of people who'd be willing to take this project on for you. With a little imagination they can yellow your teeth, make your skin more flawed, and lighten and thin your hair. The more advanced users will have no difficulty extending and deepening crows feet eyes, your frown and other tell-tell signs of ageing. In fact, this process is just reversing the doctoring taking place in magazines all the time. Print out and display in a prominent position.

Another method of considering the effects that smoking is having on you is by observing, reflecting and recording what is happening in a dairy or notebook. This idea is developed in IDEA 25, *Words on paper*.

Try another idea...

PAVEMENT PORTRAIT PAINTERS

In most large cities, shopping malls and tourists traps you can find an artist sitting behind an easel surrounded by images of James Dean, Madonna, John Wayne, Jack Nicholson, and current sporting and pop icons. Whether these drawings were actually undertaken by the artist in front of you is not a subject for this book. Most, however, can draw a flattering portrait of their sitter. Indeed, their artistic skills are usually exceeded by an ability to delude the sitter into accepting a flattering likeness.

'One only dies once, and it's for such a long time.'
MOLIÈRE

Defining idea...

Your purpose is to commission a portrait that adds a decade or two to how you look now. If the artist does not appear to understand, say that you want to see what you will look like in ten or twenty year's time.

'My face looks like a wedding cake left out in the rain.'
W.H. AUDEN

Defining idea...

53

Take your picture home and frame it, having written in large capitals the words: STOPPING SMOKING WILL SLOW DOWN THE TIME IT TAKES TO GET TO THIS. You could also photocopy it to hang in every room of your house.

How did it go?

Q   **When I want to look younger all I have to do is put on the old war paint. I'm pushing 40 and can still turn heads, so this idea seems pretty pointless for me. Tell me why I should stop?**

A   *Time marches on. All we're suggesting is that stopping smoking slows down the ravages of time. Makeup can cover up a lot of blemishes, but you're on a diminishing return. And there'll come the day when you'll have to start using a trowel to put it on.*

Q   **I did what you suggested and gave a mate of mine a digital photo which he worked on for a few hours. In the picture I look just like my mother's eldest brother. It gave me quite a shock, as he died when I was only eight. My kids thought it was really funny and suggested I get a haircut like him and start wearing his sort of clothes. Apart from providing harmless entertainment for my kids, how does this idea help?**

A   *You are what you eat; likewise, your body bears witness to everything you do to it. Without getting too high-handed, non-smokers generally wear better than smokers, and our suggestions here are a way of reminding you that you are no different from anyone else. Being reminded about someone in the family whose life was shortened by smoking is a bit of a wake-up call.*

12

Tobacco giants

Someone out there is getting very rich – at your expense – selling a deadly drug. Take a look at what's in it for the giant multinationals and the governments.

Let's talk fairy tales. As in any folk tale, there needs to be a bad guy (value for money – we have at least six). This story is set in Tobaccoland, which is ruled over by six greedy giants.

They are called British American Tobacco, Philip Morris Incorporated, R.J. Reynolds Industries, The Rembrandt Group, American Brands Inc. and Imperial Tobacco Limited. These are very, very greedy giants who don't always tell the whole truth.

Between them they rule the world. Today they have 1.3 billion subjects who all smoke their evil weed. They don't mention the 70 million people who died in the last half century from smoking, or the 100 million expected to die over the next 30 years. (Greater than the combined death tolls from AIDS, TB, traffic deaths, homicide and suicide, by the way. But they won't tell you that.)

Here's an idea for you...

Jot down your ideas for an advert for cigarettes knowing that you want people to give you as much money as possible to help them kill themselves more quickly. Send a copy to every tobacco company you can think of for comment.

NEW SLAVES FOR OLD

Unfortunately, as the slaves grew older they died early from horrible diseases. So the giants began looking to enslave the young – with any luck, these might live 30 or 40 years before they die. They also searched for new slaves in countries far beyond their borders.

Every day 90,000 new children and adolescents become their slaves. Although more than 70% of their slaves live in countries with low incomes, the giants never suggest that the money spent on the evil weed could be better spent on food or shelter, and they never think how much extra in health costs they're burdening these poor countries with.

The giants are greedy for money. Imperial Tobacco (world number 4) made £499 million profit in six months, a 32% rise from the previous year. Philip Morris (world's largest) makes in excess of £8 billion profit per year. British American Tobacco (second largest) sells over 320 brands in 180 countries; its most popular brand sold over 30 billion worldwide in 2004 and made £604 million in profits in just three months.

THE GOLDEN GOOSE

It took about 300 hundred years for the slaves to realise that the evil weed was in fact poisoning them. But by that time the giants were too strong for them to overthrow. And despite themselves, most of the slaves couldn't live without the weed.

Luckily for the giants, they found some good friends. Governments. The governments were as greedy as the giants. They saw how rich the giants had become from the evil weed and decided that they, too, wanted a share. So they made the giants give them half of everything they made from the weed.

So when the people asked their government for help, the government said no. How could they kill the goose that laid the golden egg? Some of the most important ministers in the government even took jobs with the giants, which made it very difficult for them to say anything bad about the giants. It especially meant that they weren't going to pass any laws that really harmed the giants.

And the giants were very happy. But still they needed to find more slaves to replace the ones who were dying off.

THE HANDSOME PRINCE

Then, one day, along rode a handsome young prince. He had a fine, strong horse and was an outdoor man, riding the ranges of freedom into the sunset. He was just what the giants needed. Giant Philip Morris renamed him Marlboro Man.

Try another idea...

The Tobacco Giants don't just steal your money, they can ruin your sex life as well. Check out IDEA 39, *Do you smoke after sex?*, to see how.

Defining idea...

'One of the prime activities of [the tobacco] industry is in effect to act as a tax collector for the government they will proceed very cautiously before they kill the goose which lays such a big golden egg.'
Sir DAVID NICHOLSON, Euro MP and former chairman of Rothmans International

'Tobacco addiction is a disease communicated through advertising, sports, marketing and sponsorship. This is not a free choice at all.'
GRO HARLEM BRUNDTLAND, World Health Organization

'Come to where the flavour is. Come to Marlboro country,' they said. 'Be free, be a real man like Marlboro Man,' they were saying to people. 'Take the weed and be like him.' And we believed them.

Sales of Marlboro rocketed and it became the world's leading cigarette brand, making millions. The real Marlboro Man was called Darrell Winfield. His face appeared the world over in adverts and on posters. A lifelong smoker, he died in 1976 from lung cancer. The face of Marlboro Man is still selling cigarettes worldwide.

THE GOOD GUYS COMETH

But the medical clouds were gathering and the tide was slowly turning against the evil weed. What were the giants to do? 'Everyone thinks we're bad,' they moaned (secretly). Then they had an idea. They reinvented themselves as the good guys.

Cue: fanfare. Here come the Tobacco Giants, the men who give you Formula One motor racing, soccer, tennis, snooker, cricket, art exhibitions, concerts by world-famous orchestras, sponsor university departments, put their logos on smart designer clothes and accessories, host discos and give free gifts away.

It's (cheap) advertising by stealth. We attach a feel-good factor to the Tobacco Giants for providing us with healthy pleasures (whilst forgetting their products kill). The Tobacco Giants call this the halo effect.

There's no guarantee of a halo for the millions of slaves of the weed who die.

Q **Surely our governments wouldn't allow this to happen. How can I believe this?**

A   *None of this is made up, believe me. Governments and big business need each other. Power lies with those who make the laws and those who influence them, and that's the guys at the top who make all the money by supporting each other. Go onto the web, check it out for yourself. Try www.cqct.qc.ca, www.essentialaction.org/addicted or www.inthesetimes.com/issue/25/12/washington2512, for example, or just type 'tobacco' into your search engine and explore.*

Q **The tobacco companies clearly state that their advertising only targets smokers to change brands and is not aimed at children. That's clear isn't it?**

A   *You're quite right, that's exactly what they say. So why is it that BAT sponsors discos in Beijing, giving out free samples and R.J. Reynolds hosts rock concerts with international artists in Canton, while Philip Morris stages discos in the Ukraine (entry price: five empty Marlboro packs)?*

How did it go?

59

13

Live fast, die young

Knowing how tobacco is marketed and sold might not help you give up, but at least you know where those barons are coming from.

Our heads are filled with a thousand images of how cool and sexy it is to smoke. Advertisers and movie makers know which buttons to press to turn us on. Here's how it works.

In this idea we'll consider the image the smoking industry has projected for its product, compare it with harsh reality and show you how to fight back.

Cigarette and tobacco advertising has always been brilliant. You have to admire these guys who are clearly top of their class. They could sell fridges to Eskimos or tumble dryers to the housewives living on the equator, but that's too simple for them: they need a real challenge. And selling tobacco is some challenge.

They have a product nobody really needs. Let's face it, it makes your teeth yellow, fingers brown, wrinkles your skin, messes up your fitness and costs you big time. Here's how these brilliant advertisers have responded in the past hundred years:

61

Here's an idea for you... **Start your own counter-advertising campaign. Next time you see a cigarette advert, try to mentally replace it with your counter-image Cut out photos of stars who have died of smoking-related illnesses and superimpose yellow teeth and brown fingers. Better still, find and do it to an old ad featuring Marlboro Man.**

- Get 'em young. How many people can you name who took up smoking in their thirties or beyond?
- Sell you an image.
- Blacken non-smokers' reputations.
- Associate themselves with desirable people or events.
- Cultivate an image as philanthropists and be seen to be sponsoring desirable events.
- Never say sorry or admit liability.
- Pay for 'research' that contradicts unfavourable information from the scientific community.
- Support the misguided sods who feel that restricting smoking is an infringement of their liberty.
- Always stay one step ahead of governments by using the lobby system to silence opposition.
- When sales start to decrease, move to the developing world and start again.

Let's have a look at some of these points in more detail.

Try another idea... **Now that advertisers aren't able to con you into parting with your money, you can spend it on something worthwhile. Find out how much you'll save in IDEA 14, *Money makes the world go round.***

Get 'em young. While is would be difficult to prove that cigarette barons and their advertisers actually target kids, they do go after the impressionable, which, with no disrespect to the young, is more or less the same thing.

In the early decades of the twentieth century, cigarette manufacturers were quick to sign up sports stars and attach themselves to Hollywood glamour. Even before young men were old enough to buy cigarettes for themselves they would pester parents for cigarette cards with pictures of footballers, cricketers or boxers. Forging links between cigarettes and success was a masterstroke.

'Every Marlboro ad needs to be judged on the following criteria: story value, authenticity, masculinity, while communicating those enduring core values of freedom, limitless opportunities, self-sufficiency, mastery of destiny and harmony with nature.'
Philip Morris Incorporated

Defining idea...

Reinforce this with Hollywood glamour and suddenly smoking becomes sexy as well as cool. We're not claiming that the studios were in the pocket of the tobacco barons, but tinsel town stars were and still are icons the world over, and what they do is copied everywhere. In the days when you were still allowed to smoke in cinemas, Marlene, Cary or Clark lighting up caused a knee-jerk reaction as dozens of smokers reaching for their fags and matches. Girls wanted to be like Bette Davis and boys like Humphrey Bogart or James Dean.

While we all like to believe that we're unaffected by adverts, it's still worth challenging this type of propaganda. Here are a few common messages and misconceptions followed by our counter-spin.

The adverts say...	**This is more like it...**
Smoking is sensual.	Smelling of smoke is a turn off. Don't believe us? Go and lick an ashtray.
When you smoke you look like a movie star.	You look like yourself with a cigarette in your mouth.
Non-smokers are losers.	They're richer, healthier and less wrinkly.

Smokers have more fun.	Smokers have more strokes and look on average a decade older than non-smokers.
Smoking makes you sophisticated and grown up.	Smoking makes you old before your time.
Smoking makes you more attractive.	To advertisers and cigarette barons, maybe.
You feel more confident with a cigarette.	You become more dependent on cigarettes to feel confident.
Smoking helps you relax.	Yeah, right. Try this. Take your pulse. Have a cigarette. Take your pulse again. Faster, isn't it? More relaxed? We don't think so.

How did it go?

Q   I know all the Hollywood myths are a load of hogwash, but if you burst all my dreams what will I be left with?

A   *A life, perhaps, and a slightly longer one at that. I know we're coming over as a couple of killjoys, but the cruel thing is that advertisers are effectively killing thousands of people every year and they know it.*

Q   I don't think I am influenced by cigarette advertising. Isn't it all about brand awareness anyway?

A   *That's the line the industry takes. Whenever cigarette adverts are banned, sales go down. Nobody wants to feel like a gullible schmuck, but we reckon it pays to know what you're up against.*

14

Money makes the world go round

Cigarettes are money. Your money. Up in smoke. Taxes, life insurance, you the smoker pay through the nose for your habit. Become ill and the costs spiral. Look closely at the hidden costs of smoking.

You already know the health risks and even the price of a packet of twenty, but is your habit likely to be costing you even more than you budgeted?

Cigarettes are expensive. They are especially costly in the UK, where successive chancellors have increasingly taxed smokers. While in real terms alcohol has gone down in price, cigarettes certainly haven't. Given that we live in a nanny state, the tax on cigarettes is sometimes covertly justified as a sin tax: a way of punishing you for the harm you are doing to your body and a means of making you pay for your future hospital care. And if the passive smoking lobby has its way, these taxes will rise as smokers will be expected to pay for stays in hospital and other treatments resulting from damage to lungs, heart and circulation and cancer.

Sit down with a pen and paper and someone who really knows you and work out the real cost of smoking. Be as honest as you can, taking account of as many hidden costs as possible. Having arrived at a monthly or yearly total, visualise what you would use this sum for: foreign travel, replacing the old banger or more beer.

THE BASIC COST

I started smoking when I was ... years old. I have smoked for a total of ... years, and I spend ... each week on tobacco. By totting these up you discover the staggering sum that you have handed over to supermarkets, corner shops and, indirectly, tobacco barons and the taxman since you were a teenager.

Perhaps you've already done this exercise, been shocked, then rationalised it as almost half the adult population is in the same boat. We know you're not stupid and already know how much smoking costs you each week. And if you live with a non-smoker, chances are they're already telling you how better the money could be spent (on them, perhaps?). You already know you can't go anywhere without either a packet of ten or money for more.

'Our objective is to maximize prices, such that we exceed cost base increases, while avoiding undesired margin scrutiny by the authorities whenever threatened.' Philip Morris Incorporated, internal memo

LITTLE ADD ONS

There's no easy way to say this, but the harsh truth is even worse. And this is even if you make allowances for the reality that most of us smoke – or drink – more than we probably think we do. Here's a list of indirect ways smoking hits your pocket:

■ Life insurance: either companies offer smokers a higher premium or give non-smokers a discount. It boils down to the same thing: puffers pay more.

■ Extra dry-cleaning bills. If you smoke, your suits and other clothes will need to be washed or dry cleaned more frequently than if you don't.

■ Redecoration: if you want to see the effect smoking has on the paintwork, just walk into a pub. Non-smoking households stay fresher longer.

■ Cover ups: peppermints, air fresheners.

■ Expensive alternatives: you are out for the evening. Usually you buy cigarettes at the supermarket. You have run out. Do you (a) tell yourself it's a fair cop and you'll wait until you get home or (b) go to the vending machine and buy a packet of seventeen at a third more than you normally pay for twenty?

■ Specialist products: normal toothpaste doesn't do the job smoker's toothpaste does. True, but how much more does smoker's toothpaste cost?

In reality, these concrete examples only take you to the foothills of what your addiction actually costs. If time is money, how much have you lost in cigarette breaks both at home and work? Time that could have been more productively spent. More and more employees are being promoted based on energy, zeal and ability to keep the nose to the grindstone. Give your boss the impression that you are always popping out for a cigarette break and you

Smoking has an impact on your health as well as your pocket. Check out IDEA 28, *No respecter of reputations*, for information about famous people killed by smoking.

Try another idea...

'*I thought I couldn't afford to take her out and smoke as well. So I gave up cigarettes. Then I took her out and one day I looked at her and thought: 'Oh well,' and I went back to smoking again, and that was better.*'
BENNY HILL, comedian who lived and died alone.

Defining idea...

might just get passed over for a vital promotion to the benefit of a keen upstart who is seen as more productive. And if the habit results in reduced health and fitness, what price then? And if smoking shortens your life – and it's reckoned that one in two smokers dies of a smoking-related illness – you will have paid the ultimate price.

How did it go?

Q   I get really sick of people telling me how much my habit costs me. As it happens, I travel abroad a fair bit and bring back duty-free cigarettes all the time. Along with the ones other people get me, I hardly need to buy any at home. How can I benefit from this idea?

A   *I'm delighted that you have found a way of avoiding paying cigarette duty. However, although your cigarettes may cost you less than other smokers pay, it's still a hell of a lot more than non-smokers pay. This is even before you consider the indirect costs.*

Q   I have no way of knowing how much it costs me to smoke. My partner and I both smoke and we buy for both of us. I don't even know who smokes more. How can I find out?

A   *Why not do the exercise jointly? It's both your money, after all.*

15

Using the wrong time to do the right thing

You really want to quit, tomorrow. But then there's that little voice in your head reminding you that tomorrow never comes.

Waiting until you feel completely committed to giving up is as futile as looking for Mr or Ms Right on the moon.

Almost everyone wants to give up smoking sometimes: admittedly, a time other than now. It could be for any number of reasons: cost, health grounds, effect on physical appearance, to silence a disapproving partner, stigma, a cocktail of any of these reasons or quirky ones only you know about.

If this is true, it should follow that more people ought to be giving up than actually are. That is, until you take account of harsh reality: that in the short term at least the benefits of stopping are outweighed by the urge to put off quitting just a little longer. This is a natural and totally understandable human trait. We are programmed not only to avoid pain or discomfort, but also to defer it as long as possible.

Ambivalence about stopping means that most of us put all the good reasons for wanting to give up on the back burner and use its flame to light up what we kid

Here's an idea for you... **Start to track setbacks and other disappointments so that you can muster enough bad temper and feeling to quit. We reckon you won't have to wait long before the feel-bad factor grows sufficiently for you to stop.**

ourselves will be one of our last cigarettes. The time to stop, we tell ourselves, is not quite now: tomorrow I will feel stronger about quitting; I will have more motivation and will be less likely to buckle under.

Which brings us to a profoundly important sentence:

THE BEST TIME TO QUIT SMOKING IS WHEN YOU'RE FEELING SHIT

This simple statement might sound counter-intuitive – arse about face to the rest of us – but think back to those times when anger gave you the energy and concentration to carry out a job you would otherwise avoid: sorting out the junk in the garage, your files or the sock drawer, or doing the washing up.

THE BEST TIME TO QUIT SMOKING IS WHEN YOU'RE FEELING SHIT

Rather than wait for that perfect day when the sun shines and you wake up to find the desire to smoke has vanished while you were in the Land of Nod, here, in no particular order, are our top ten excuses to give up:

- You've been sacked and have lost your job.
- A serious relationship has broken down and you or your partner has walked out.
- There is a death on the family.
- You've been in an RTA (road traffic accident).
- Your home has been broken into and you hadn't renewed the insurance.

- Your team gets relegated.
- The party you didn't vote for gets re-elected.
- You get passed over for a much-hoped-for and (at least in your eyes) deserved promotion.
- Your son or daughter starts experimenting with crack cocaine.
- You or your partner has an unplanned pregnancy/can't get pregnant.

One great way of not procrastinating is setting a quit date which is reinforced by a change of scenery. If you turn to IDEA 44, *Trial separation*, you can read our suggestions for quitting away from family or colleagues.

Try another idea...

One of the great things about using disappointments, disasters and setbacks, major or minor, to fuel your ambition to give up is that they generally come along at reasonable intervals. On the other hand, if you just wait for success to arrive you might be waiting forever.

Luckily major setbacks don't come along that often, so it worth exploring minor disappointments and difficulties. Here are ten of our nominations:

'Thank heaven I have given up smoking again!...God I feel fit. Homicidal but fit. A different man. Irritable, moody, depressed, rude, nervy, perhaps; but the lungs are fine.'
A. P. HERBERT

Defining idea...

1. You lock yourself out of the house and your partner and only other key is a two hour drive away.

2. You break a fingernail.

3. A navy blue sock is left in the washing machine prior to the white wash.

4. A cluster of fresh spots has appeared on your face.

5. You've lost your wallet or handbag, but it might still be at home.

6. It's your partner's birthday, but you've forgotten to buy a present. A homemade card with a pledge to quit might get you out of jail.

7. Under your windscreen wiper a parking ticket is waiting.

8. The electricity bill arrives and is a lot more than expected.

9. The telephone is on the blink.

10. You reverse the family runabout into a concrete bollard in the supermarket car park.

Defining idea...

'Cigarettes are killers that travel in packs.'
Anon.

Oh, and don't forget, THE BEST TIME TO QUIT SMOKING IS WHEN YOU'RE FEELING SHIT.

Q   **I just don't get this. Up till now I have used my cigs as a buffer to cushion hurt and disappointment. Isn't throwing them away only going to make things even worse?**

How did it go?

A   *To be brutally frank with you, yes. Most smokers find it painful to stop and nicotine is the first drug they turn to. But this particular pain barrier can be surmounted, and there is a real pleasure to be had from knowing that you have the willpower and guts to resist taking the easy way out.*

Q   **I've tried using this method, and it works up to a point. I get really pissed off about something, throw all the cigarettes out of the house and promise myself that's it. After a while I calm down and before I know it I'm on my hands and knees rooting around the shrubbery for my lost smokes and life is back to normal. What am I doing wrong?**

A   *You're not doing anything wrong. It seems to us that you need another quitting strategy to sustain your efforts. Have you considered patches or other forms of nicotine replacement therapy?*

16

Diversion ahead

Discovering ploys that help you distract yourself from cravings can prevent a relapse.

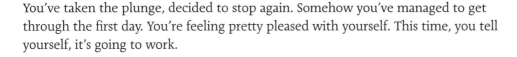

However strong your resolve, you can't give up the weed by willpower alone. Following our diversions can keep you moving in the right direction.

You've taken the plunge, decided to stop again. Somehow you've managed to get through the first day. You're feeling pretty pleased with yourself. This time, you tell yourself, it's going to work.

Sooner rather than later the craving comes: 'Just one little ciggie,' the sirens call, 'one cigarette won't make a difference and it will make you feel a whole lot better.' You're tempted. Maybe these thoughts are triggered by a setback, a petty frustration or a minor disappointment, or it might be that you find yourself doing something or being somewhere where you'd usually be lighting up: after a meal perhaps? After sex? Being in the company of cigarette-smoking companions? The cravings come knocking like an uninvited friend – unexpectedly, if you have not tried to give up before, or with the unpleasant familiarity of a landlord coming for his rent if you are a serial stopper.

Here's an idea for you...

Produce a table with three columns, describing the times and circumstances that you smoke; your reasons for smoking then; and alternative (non-smoking) ways of getting the same result. Recruit the help of your partner or someone who knows you well. Be as honest as you can. When thinking of the non-smoking alternatives, try to be as creative as possible, bearing in mind lifestyle limitations, but make sure that they are achievable, sustainable and, most importantly, not punitive.

Can cravings be stopped? NO.

Can you learn to cope with them and continue to quit using strategies that have worked for others? Quite possibly YES.

How?

In a nutshell, you need to be prepared for precipitators that urge you to light up and plan how you are going to deal with them. You can deal with them in three stages.

Stage one
List the times and places, people and events that usually result in you lighting up.

Stage two
Beside each cigarette-smoking occasion you've listed, describe the reasons why you smoke at that particular time.

Try another idea...

Want to know more about the gratification that drives your impulse to start smoking again? IDEA 33, *I want it now*, will tell you.

Stage three
Describe a non-smoking alternative.

Here's one we did earlier

Clive's chart

Cigarette	Reason	Alternative actions
First thing in the morning	I'm gasping for one. I can stand outside the house and contemplate the day ahead. My wife and daughter are not bothering me and someone else will answer the phone.	I can go for a walk. I can still use this time to think through problems alone and mentally prepare myself for the day. I will experiment with gum or fruit to see if it helps.
After meetings	Haven't had a cig for up to 90 minutes. I can get away from what often seems an intense environment. I can use the time to reflect on what has happened and preparing my exit strategy. I enjoy the banter you get with other smokers and relating to them in an informal environment. I have an excuse to leave the room for a cigarette which gives me time to check my mobile and respond to pressing issues from the office.	

'I phoned my dad to tell him I had stopped smoking. He called me a quitter.'
STEVEN PEARL

Defining idea...

Post-lunch puffs	Rounds off the meal nicely. Provides an interlude before the washing up. Gives me more thinking time.	Another walk, perhaps. Will experiment with changing midday mealtime. Leave washing up till the evening.
After an argument	This cigarette helps me calm down.	Attempt to stay with awful feelings with or without the other person and see what happens.
When I'm thinking about doing something unpleasant	A cig gives me thinking time and delays putting off something I dread.	Talk it through with colleagues or write down pros and cons for taking this action if it can't be shared with others.
After I've done something unpleasant	Helps me calm down. Reward for doing something I hate having to do.	Buy myself a present.

Defining
idea...

'Defeat does not finish a man, quitting does. A man is not finished when he's defeated. He's finished when he quits.'
RICHARD M. NIXON

Q   **I've had a look at Clive's chart and am impressed at his honesty, especially about the need to smoke outside to get way from other members of his family. If I wrote this down it would cause an awful scene. Can you help?**

How did it go?

A   *Writing in code would keep it safe from all prying eyes. After all, Samuel Pepys's diary code didn't get cracked until 123 years after his death. Alternatively, you could just ensure that other family members don't get a chance to see it. For example, my sock drawer is a pretty forbidding place.*

Q   **Putting a name on different cigarettes strikes me as daft. I'm just hooked and that's it. Can you convince me otherwise?**

A   *Maybe it is daft, but we reckon that if you asked a good friend they are almost certain to be able to predict certain times or occasions when you will light up. Go on, just try it out for a laugh. You could also ask yourself 'Why am I lighting up now?' It should be a revealing exercise.*

17

Suck it and see

Fancy doubling your chances of becoming an ex-smoker? There's scientific proof that nicotine replacement therapy (NRT) does just that.

Help is at hand. Nicotine replacement gum, patches, sprays etc. are all readily available at the chemist's or on prescription.

While you may have started smoking for reasons that only you will know, we reckon we know why you and everyone else continues to light up morning, noon and night, day in and day out: an addiction to nicotine. Cigarettes have just become the means of getting your fix of this drug into your body.

The good news is that a variety of alternatives methods have been devised to get you your nicotine fix in ways that can break the link with cigarettes and can wean you off the weed. These methods are not so much alternatives to cigarettes as ways to regulate the amount of nicotine your body needs while it is reducing its dependency on this highly addictive drug. Get it right and the withdrawal symptoms should be minimal. These products are not cheap and can work out as expensive as smoking even on prescription, but given that you will only need to use them for about three months, it is worth thinking of them as a wise investment.

Here's an idea for you...

Wherever you live there is likely to be a smoking cessation service not too far away that offers either individual or group therapy. In the UK these services are often run by the NHS. Check one out and see what advice and support it offers for people wishing to try NRT.

CHEW IT OVER

Nicotine chewing gum is great because it gives you a nicotine fix where and when you need it. Like all these alternatives, you have the additional advantage that you are not restricted to using designated smoking areas in public places and can get the relief you need wherever you happen to be. Your body takes in nicotine through your gums as you chew. We know it might sound obvious, but if you chew all the time, you'll get a steady flow of nicotine, which, unless you chain smoke all day every day, isn't the same as the intermittent nicotine fixes you get from smoking. The way round this is to rest nicotine gum in your cheek from time to time. And don't swallow, as you can't absorb it like this and it gets wasted. The gum comes is different flavours, such as juicy fruit and mint, and in different strengths. It is best to think of the gum as a medication to be taken on the hour, ever hour and should be taken for the prescribed period. In practice it is easy to be lured into a false sense of security and skip the gum after a while as the cravings disappear, only to find the old urge to pop out for a quick one resurfacing.

PATCHWORK

Nicotine patches give you a constant flow of nicotine through your skin. Shop around, as some look really noticeable but others are barely visible. It's a good idea to move them to a different patch of skin every day so that they don't provoke a skin reaction. Patches come in 16 and 24 hour versions. Unless you usually get up in the middle of the night for a smoke, 16 hour patches are the way to go.

DOWN THE HATCH

If gum's not your style and you want to bare all this summer without showing everyone you're trying to beat your addiction with patches (or you want an all-over tan), microtabs could be just the thing. These little tablets dissolve under your tongue. All you need to do is hold one under your tongue until it fizzles away to nothing. If you suck, chew or swallow, you'll dwindle the dose and the drugs won't work. Some people particularly like this method as they enjoy the big hit the tablets provide.

SMOKE SWEETS

If you really can't resist sucking your microtabs, ditch them in favour of nicotine lozenges. Just don't chew.

SNIFF, SNIFF

For a few hardcore smokers, most forms of nicotine replacement just aren't quite strong enough. Think you might fall into this group? Put those sniffs of shame to good use by using a nicotine nasal spray. It's the strongest form of nicotine replacement out there, and as the nicotine is absorbed through the lining of your nose, it works very quickly. Perfect for those monster withdrawal pangs and you also get a great hit from this product.

If you think that NRT is for wimps and you fancy fronting out the monster without this sort of help, why not check out IDEA 18, *Cold turkey*, and see how far you can go?

Try another idea...

'A cigarette is the perfect type of a perfect pleasure. It is exquisite and it leaves one unsatisfied. What more can one want?'
OSCAR WILDE, *The Picture of Dorian Gray*

Defining idea...

'Nicotine patches are great. Stick one over each eye and you can't find your cigarettes.'
Anon.

Defining idea...

83

Q You might think I'm being silly, but I'm worried that nicotine patches will give me skin cancer. Am I right?

A   *You're not being silly, no, but you'll be pleased to know that the nicotine in NRT does not cause cancer.*

Q When I've tried to give up before, one of the things I miss is the feeling of having a cigarette in my hand. I've never been into chewing gum and anyway it's not the same. What do you suggest?

A   *You're not alone in this. Fortunately, they've thought of an answer: inhalators. You might have seen them being used: they are made of white plastic, are about the same size and shape as a cigarette and you can use them to suck in nicotine. They should be readily available from pharmacies.*

Q My sister's pregnant and knows that continuing to smoke will harm her baby so has cut down. Could she use patches or gum instead, or are they too unsafe in pregnancy?

A   *We suggest that your sister gets advice about this from her family doctor. But any form of nicotine replacement ought to be safer than smoking, as her unborn baby will be exposed to less carbon monoxide and many other poisons.*

18

Cold turkey

A short, sharp shock or a phased withdrawal? A case can be made either way.

Giving up instantly works for some. It's a hard road to take, but the agony isn't drawn out. So, which suits you — stop dead or cut down gradually? We look at the pros and cons.

Think back to your days at school. Swimming lessons in early spring or late autumn. It may not be literally freezing, but with the chill factor it certainly feels it. The pool is outdoors and it's unheated. Given that you haven't got a hope in hell of getting out of the lesson, do you (a) put off full immersion as long as possible, dipping one foot in and quickly withdrawing it, then slowly increasing the amount of your goose-pimpled body you exposed to the cold, or (b) dive in and get the traumatic business over with in one unpleasant hit? Maybe you tried both methods before deciding which approach suited you better. There's a lot to be said for those brave souls who go for broke: in no time at all they have got used to the water, while the procrastinators (or wimps, as the brave souls keep calling them) on the edge or in the shallow end are still suffering.

That knowledge might indicate whether you're temperamentally better suited to cold turkey or gradual cessation of smoking, but if you're still not sure, here are a few pointers to help inform your choice.

Here's an idea for you...

You've gone cold turkey and are over the worst. Great. Why not celebrate by throwing a post-smoking party? It is reckoned to take thirty days to create a new habit of not smoking, so book a date a month after you've given up and use the occasion to thank your support team for getting you through the worst.

PROS OF COLD TURKEY

- It's a clean break. You and other people know where you are. Once you have set a date and have shared it with the important people in your life, you can be regarded as a non-smoker sending out clear messages that you don't want to be offered a smoke or given any encouragement to resume.
- Within an hour of stopping, your blood pressure falls, your lungs start clearing out mucus and your breathing becomes easier.
- You can throw out ashtrays, lighters and everything to do with your old habit. Having to replace these things might just put the brakes on your waning resolve.
- Going out for a meal, cold turkeys can be directed to the non-smoking section of a restaurant.
- You can enjoy your last cigarette, whereas if you were only cutting down every cigarette you had would be tinged with guilt.
- You will get all your unpleasant symptoms over in one hit. You can make harm limitation contingencies to help you over the hump.
- Faced with withdrawal symptoms, people who attempt to cut down often self-medicate by lighting up again. Not a problem for cold turkeys.
- Your body knows what's happening. Bodies find it hard to cope with being in a state of limbo: you either have cancer or are in remission; dead or alive. Smoker or non-smoker.

Try another idea...

Want to make a clean break but can never find the right time? IDEA 15, *Using the wrong time to do the right thing*, suggests ways of finding motivation to quit.

- Cutting down is a bit like HP – hire purchase –you never get to the final payment, and it costs you a lot more in the process.
- Withdrawal symptoms apart, you start to get the benefits of being a non-smoker from day one. Increased fitness, more energy, breathing fresher air, cleaner clothes, more disposable income: the list is endless.

Want to give up but prefer to chicken out of cold turkey? Check out IDEA 17, *Suck it and see,* **for our thoughts on nicotine replacement patches, sprays and gum**

Try another idea...

CONS OF COLD TURKEY

- It's a shock to the system that is just too much for some people. This might be more psychological than physical, but its still too much to cope with.
- Suddenly stopping can make some people impossible to live with. They are so dependent on cigarettes that withdrawal means they have to turn to another vice – usually alcohol – which makes their nearest and dearest plead for them to start smoking again.

'I know a man who gave up smoking, drinking, sex, and rich food. He was healthy right up to the day he killed himself.'
JOHNNY CARSON

Defining idea...

On balance, cold turkey has lots going for it. People who are giving up are still smokers while cold turkeys, even after only a day or two, can consider themselves ex-smokers. You are starting to breath in clean sweet air, can send your best togs to the dry cleaners and start getting positive vibes back from your support team. It's only the start of the journey along a road strewn with hazards and obstacles, but it could be a new beginning.

'To smoke or not to smoke: I can make of either a life-work.'
MIGNON MCLAUGHLIN

Defining idea...

87

How did it go?

Q **I've been trying a mixture of both methods for the past ten years to no avail. But whether I'm cutting down or staying off, my resolve always breaks down pretty damned quickly. What do you suggest?**

A *You are not alone. And the more you tell everyone you're trying to cut down or have given up, the less they believe you. If, as in your case, giving up is easy to talk about and seemingly impossible to follow through with, we think you need to have a rethink. Maybe you need just one person to talk to, say your partner, and a written plan identifying a starting date, inducements to continue and rewards to celebrate getting past important milestones: first day, first week, first difficult day, Christmas and so on.*

Q **I've been smoking since I was fourteen. That was thirty-five years ago. Surely going cold turkey would be more than my body could stand?**

A *You might find it reassuring to know that the opposite is true: cold turkey will do you a lot more good than continuing to smoke. Admittedly, you can't undo the damage smoking has already inflicted on your body, but stopping smoking will prevent things from getting worse as well as reducing the risks of anything else going wrong. It will be a shock to your body, but just think of the money you'll save.*

19

Super drugs

Discover a drug that effectively curbs cravings and reduces withdrawals.

Medication may be the answer when everything else has failed, or even before.

Bupropion hydrochloride was originally developed as an antidepressant, but has since been found to have other effects. It goes by a couple of other names: amfebutamone is it's official European title, Wellbutrin in the States, and you might also come across it by it's trade name, Zyban.

Although bupropion was being used as an antidepressant when doctors discovered it reduced nicotine withdrawal symptoms, you definitely don't have to be depressed to use it, and if it works you won't be depressed afterwards either. It's important that we're up-front and make it clear that it won't eliminate all your withdrawal symptoms – but it will make them weaker. So much so that many people are blissfully unaware of them. Where it really comes into its own is with cravings, which are drastically reduced. It's totally different from nicotine gum, patches and other replacement therapy, because it doesn't contain any nicotine. And, unlike nicotine replacement therapy, you can only get it on prescription.

Here's an idea for you...

You've set your quit date. That's brilliant. Now make another date, this time with your doctor, to talk through the pros and cons of bupropion and work out the best time to start taking it.

SMOKING SCIENCE

Here's how it works.

Make a date

Sadly, this isn't the sort of tablet you can take once and forget about while it does its stuff.

Before starting it, you need to set and commit to a stop date. You'll need to take it for at least eight weeks and you stop smoking in the second week. Here's how it goes:

- You'll start taking one tablet of 150 mg bupropion a week before your stop date. This is to make sure a decent amount of drug is active in your bloodstream by the time you stop.
- In the day or so leading up to your start date, your doctor will probably advise you to increase your daily dose to two tablets, so you're getting a total of 300 mg bupropion.
- You'll continue to take two tablets (300 mg bupropion) for the next seven to eleven weeks, depending on your doctor's advice.

Defining idea...

'I was really ill on Zyban, I was sick all the time, my ankles swelled up making it painful to walk. Never again.'
CLIVE HOPWOOD, author, ageing hippy and Renaissance man

Why a drug?

Nicotine addiction is a disease. Stopping could save your life.

Dead Serious

In the UK, out of 513,000 people who have taken bupropion, fifty-eight have died taking it. In Canada to date there have been over a thousand reports of serious side effects, including 172 people who had fits and nineteen who died.

Experts haven't been able to prove that bupropion has caused these deaths. It may be that they died because of smoking-related illnesses they had already. As with any drug, different people can get different side effects. We are aware of people who complain of

If you think that this sort of drug is for wimps and want to use sheer willpower, go to IDEA 18, *Cold turkey*, and take it from there.

Try another idea...

disturbed sleep or bodily pains. Having said that, it doesn't take too much to suppose that if you've got a serious smoking-related illness like lung cancer or heart disease you need to stop smoking fast, so you are both more likely to take buprioion and more likely to die of your illness.

The bottom line
There are pros and cons to taking any drug, and we'd recommend a visit to your doctor to weigh up the bupropion balance.

You definitely shouldn't take it if:

- You have fits, or have had them in the past.
- You have an eating disorder (like bulimia or anorexia nervosa).
- You are taking a drug called a monoamine oxidase inhibitor.
- You have recently stopped hitting the bottle, taking prescription tranquilisers or cut ties with your drug dealer. Stopping many kinds of drugs, prescribed or otherwise procured, can crank up your pulse and cause other physical symptoms which make it more risky to take bupropion.

'I went on Zyban about two years ago and it worked for me. I didn't have any side effects at all. It just made you forget to smoke. I have the occasional cigarette now but I'll never go back to fifteen a day and there's never getting up at two in the morning to have one.'
MARTIN CHEUNG, computer engineer and former smoker

Defining idea...

How did it go?

Q **I'm pregnant and am desperate to give up. I've tried (and failed) numerous other ways of stopping, but none of them have worked for me. Could taking this medication be the answer?**

A *Sadly, no. You can't use bupropion hydrochloride while you are pregnant or breast feeding, as it hasn't been shown to be safe. Why not ask your family doctor about nicotine replacement therapy?*

Q **Why can't I buy these tablets over the counter? After all, I'll be taking them to stop me smoking, which everyone keeps telling me is a killer.**

A *You've made a really valid point, but we are dealing with serious stuff here. This drug needs to be prescribed and monitored, and there are some people who it could be really bad news for. For instance, if you take it, there's about a one in a thousand chance of your having an epileptic fit, so if you've ever had fits, have had a head injury or are a heavy drinker then it's not for you. We know it sounds a bit pedantic and stuffy, but it's for these and other reasons that this medication must be taken under medical supervision.*

Q **I'm a heavy smoker and also suffer from depression. Do other antidepressants have the same effect on cravings?**

A *Being depressed can deplete your willpower and motivation, so we're impressed you're reading this and have made an important step towards becoming a non-smoker. Yes, other antidepressants, especially a drug called nortryptiline, have been shown to help in much the same way, but at the moment bupropion is the only one that's licensed as a smoking cessation drug.*

20

Smoke screen

This is the time the addict in you is going to start getting worried. And the time he'll start pulling out his dirtiest tricks. A handy guide to all the subtle games the addict will play on you to get you to give up giving up. Don't be fooled!

Meet the Tobacco Demon. And he's far more deadly than Nicotine Nick. Beating the nicotine addiction is the easy bit. Unravelling and defeating the psychological web of addiction beneath is a tougher task.

If you know the movie *Forbidden Planet*, you'll know that there is a terrifying creature that threatens everyone's life. But it's not real, it feeds off the mind of the main character. The Tobacco Demon is a bit like him. He feeds off you.

The Demon feels like a real and ominously powerful enemy. But he's inside your head, a creation of your own making. He comes as part of every smoking addict's kit. He, far more than the poison nicotine, keeps you being a smoker.

Here's an idea for you... **Write a letter to every tobacco company. Tell them you are addicted to cigarettes and you think that it may be bad for your health. Ask their advice on how to stop.**

BEWARE OF THE DEMON

When you've overcome the serious cravings for a cigarette, and are feeling pleased with yourself, you'll need to be on your guard against the Demon. He never, ever goes away because he's part of you. He can waylay you years later.

He comes across as a sympathetic friend who understands you, the smoker. He readily agrees that it's hard to give up smoking (so why bother?). He's aware that smoking is bad for you (so why not just cut down a bit?). He knows it's difficult to stay stopped (so why not just have one?).

He's a selfish liar. He wants you to stay an addict, not stop. He'll come up with a thousand excuses for why you don't need to do it now (wait until you're 'ready'). He'll support all your reasons for how stopping smoking will make life more difficult – you'll get irritable, you'll become fat, all your friends still smoke…

He's always ready with an answer. And the solution is always have a cigarette.

SMOKE OUT THE ENEMY WITHIN

The Tobacco Demon is a parasite and he'll kill you in the end. You need to know your enemy within and sever the hold he has over you.

The Demon is clever, he's subtle, he could charm the birds out of the trees. But he's not your friend, he's your murderer. Don't give him house room. Throw him out with the garbage, where he belongs. Chain him up. Destroy him.

His one and only idea is SMOKE, but he has a million brilliant ideas for why it's a good idea. Don't believe him. Every idea he has is wrong, they're all lies. Don't forget, he works for the Tobacco Giants.

There are plenty of alternatives to smoking. Look at IDEA 16, *Diversion ahead*, for some great ideas.

Try another idea...

WEAPONS OF MASS DESTRUCTION

Forget Saddam Hussein and his forty-five-minute missiles. Cigarettes are the big lie and the single most avoidable cause of death in the western world. The Tobacco Demon can deliver his deadly weapons within seconds, just as long as it takes to get you to reach for the pack and light up.

Whenever you get that urge, stop. Stop for ten seconds. Think what you're doing. If you've picked up any of the Brilliant Ideas here, go for it and use your defences – nicotine gum, meditation, whatever it is. Pause for thought and save your life.

THE USUAL SUSPECTS

The Tobacco Demon feeds off all the mini-habits and rituals that make up your smoking. They are your weaknesses, and he haunts them day and night. Know your weak spots, the moments when you're most vulnerable; be on the lookout for the Demon. He'll be there, you can be sure.

'Tobacco that outlandish weede
It spends the braine and spoiles the seede
It dulls the spirite, it dims the sight
It robs a woman of her right.'
WILLIAM VAUGHAN, poet and colonial pioneer

Defining idea...

Defining idea...

'Our business is to produce quality tobacco products. Statistics show that smokers are far more likely to develop lung cancer and certain other diseases. We believe that no one should regard cigarettes as safe.'
Imperial Tobacco website, 2005

Round up your usual suspects, the ones that act as triggers for you to smoke, and you'll know the obvious places to find the Demon. But he's not your common or garden enemy. He hides in places where you'll least expect to find him. And he always feels like he's your friend, he's here to help you, he understands you.

When we decide to give up, all of us are uncertain whether we can do it. If you've tried before and failed, that uncertainty can undermine your self-belief. The Demon knows this and probes for the moments when you're feeling low on confidence. Follow these five simple hints to defeat him.

1. Having decided to quit, learn this mantra: I don't smoke, I don't smoke.

2. Never smoke that first cigarette. Ever.

3. Tell yourself: I'm not a slave, I'm stronger than the Tobacco Demon. I don't want to feed the greedy Tobacco Giants.

4. Repeat: I want to live for me, my children. If I smoke, I'm dead.

5. And again: The Demon will always be around when I least expect him. I'll always be ready.

Destroy the Tobacco Demon and health, wealth and happiness can be yours.

Q **I keep hoping that the cost is going to persuade me to beat my Demon but the price of a packet of cigarettes make no difference to me. The price keeps going up but I keep buying them anyway. Saving money by stopping doesn't interest me, so where will I find a reason to stop?**

How did it go?

A *The real cost is your health. The choice is life or death.*

Q **I'd love to give up, but I just don't think I have the willpower. What can I do?**

A *You do have the willpower, believe me. You just have to find the right way to channel it. Millions of people have done it before, and they're no better than you. There are loads of ways to support your desire to quit. You can do it. Even if you try and fail, try again and again. You'll win in the end, no question.*

21

The air that we breathe

Medical science can do miracles these days. So that means I can carry on abusing my body and by the time I need it they'll have come up with some cunning cure. So, can we measure you for your wheelchair now, sir?

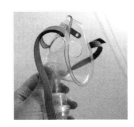

Simple fact: without air we die. Of course, we can get by on less air, but it makes the heart work much harder and it can be a painful experience. So, given it's such an essential for life, how can anyone in their right mind choose to screw up their airways?

We smokers can and do every time we light up. Though we're probably not in our right minds, of course.

NEW LUNGS FOR OLD

Every time we breathe in, our lungs absorb the oxygen from the air and expel the carbon dioxide from our body. The oxygen is absorbed into our bloodstream and is distributed to the muscles as fuel. The carbon dioxide, which is the spent fuel, is transported back to the lungs and expelled.

Here's an idea for you...

Take a slightly damp tissue. Light a cigarette and draw the smoke into your mouth. Then, without inhaling, breathe all your smoke out directly through the tissue. Repeat until you've finished the cigarette. This is what goes into your lungs every time you light up.

When we smoke, the tar from the burning cigarette enters our airways through our mouth and throat, then travels down the oesophagus into the lungs, which branch out into ever smaller passages ready for the blood to absorb the life-giving oxygen. But this tar that we send down with every lungful of smoke steadily coats everything in a black sticky slime. Oxygen has great difficulty breaking through it, with the result that smokers get 15% less oxygen than everyone else. And the heart has to crank up its action to keep everything working.

Eventually the build-up of tar will become so great that breathing becomes really difficult and as a result we become less mobile. 'I'd walk a mile for a Camel,' said a famous 1920s advertising slogan for R.J. Reynolds. Unfortunately, smoke enough of them – or any other cigarette – and you'll be hard pressed to walk a yard, let alone a mile.

LOW TAR, NO TAR

There's no such thing as a safe cigarette, so it's no use fooling ourselves – despite what tobacco companies say – that one cigarette is less hazardous than another. It's rather like choosing to be run down by a bus or a lorry: either way, the outcome for you is not good.

Defining idea...

'In Britain about 90% of all lung cancer and emphysema is caused by smoking, and about 20% of coronary heart disease.'
MARTIN RAW, *Kick the Habit*

Cigarettes were originally sold unfiltered. When filters were introduced the idea was broadcast that not only did they improve the flavour, but they also filtered out many of the harmful effects. They don't. The filter reduces the amount of smoke and helps convince you that you're not setting fire to your lungs and filling them with muck, that's about all.

Consider what our cigarette smoke does to others in IDEA 31, *Shared air*.

Try another idea...

The tar from a cigarette is generated by the burning of the tobacco and paper. That transfers directly to your lungs via the smoke. Although there may be a difference in taste between a 'full flavour' cigarette and a 'light' and a difference in the tar yield, it makes no real difference to their comparative safety. No cigarette is safe – they'll all kill you.

SAFER SMOKING?

There's no such thing as safer smoking. The only safe way to smoke is not to. You can make a very tiny difference by not smoking the cigarette down to the end or taking fewer puffs, but that's really a con. You'll probably just end up smoking two or three extra cigarettes to make up for it, so you're no better off.

'"Don't smoke" is advice hard for patients to swallow. May we suggest instead "Smoking Philip Morris?" Tests showed three out of every four cases of smoker's cough cleared on changing to Philip Morris. Why not observe the results for yourself?'
Philip Morris Incorporated advert, 1943

Defining idea...

You wouldn't run into a poison gas chamber and try to breathe, so why smoke? If you smoke in your car you'll know what a foul-smelling place it is. Paul Skerritt, President of Australian Medical Association Western Australia, describes being in a car full of smoke as 'like being locked up in a mobile gas chamber'. He's got a point.

Don't fool yourself. There is no get-out clause. Smoking kills and that's that. Damage your lungs and you'll destroy your body.

How did
it go?

Q   **I find myself coughing violently first thing in the morning. Should I change to a low-tar brand?**

A   *Listen carefully to what your body's trying to tell you. By smoking you're introducing deadly poisons and burning hot smoke into your system. This isn't natural, and your body knows it. When you cough in the morning your body is doing its level best to expel all the alien gunk you're pushing into it. Your body knows best. A low-tar cigarette will still make you cough – your body does not want cigarettes.*

Q   **I've been smoking for 20 years, although only quite moderately. I have quite a sedentary job and drive to work. I've been finding myself out of breath climbing stairs recently or doing physical things. Would it help if I cut down on my cigarettes?**

A   *Smoking less has always got to be a good thing. The longer you carry on smoking, however, the more danger you put yourself in. It's 4.5 times more dangerous to smoke 10 cigarettes a day for 20 years than it is to smoke 20 a day for 10 years. Sounds too as if you could do with more exercise to improve your fitness. Cut down on the cigarettes or, better still, stop altogether and you'll be surprised how quickly your body will show signs of recovery.*

22

Don't do that, do this

The thought of cold turkey ruffles you. Nicotine patches don't cover it. And gum just won't stick. Why not look at some of the alternative methods that may be all you need to quit while you're ahead (and still alive)?

You may feel that so-called 'new age' treatments are not for you. Most of the treatments available, however, have been around for aeons — far longer than cigarettes — and are founded on ancient wisdoms.

Ask around and see if any of your friends have tried any alternative methods. For some people they're the perfect answer. Treatment can sometimes be pricey, but if you give up smoking you'll make your money back in no time.

QUICK FIXES

Never thought you'd be sticking a needle in yourself to stop being a drug addict? Acupuncture has the painless answer. Tackle the addiction, relieve stress, improve your sleep patterns. Those needles have a point.

Acupuncture works on a pattern of energy lines running through the body which have key points, like junctions in a power system. Tap into these and you can

Here's an idea for you... **Join a gym or take up a regular exercise routine. Working your body triggers the release of endorphins into your bloodstream, which creates a natural high.**

change the flow of energy. Its a system of medicine that's used in a whole range of conditions. In some parts of the world it's even used as a substitute for anaesthetics in surgery. And it works.

In treating smoking, acupuncture works on the principle that changing the energy flow can provide valuable assistance in reducing both your craving and the tensions that come with giving up. It's not at all painful, despite how it looks. Acupuncture is widely used in helping heroin users get off the drug.

The secret is to choose the right practitioner, and the best bet here is to go by recommendation. If all else fails, look for a complementary or alternative medicine centre near you.

LOOK INTO MY EYES

Sneak up on your habit and tackle it while it's not looking with hypnosis. Talking to your subconscious could help root out the underlying causes of your addiction and give you hidden support.

Hypnosis is absolutely harmless and relaxes you to a point somewhere between being asleep and awake, rather like how you feel as you are just drifting off to sleep.

Defining idea... **'More doctors smoke camels than any other cigarette!'**
R.J. Reynolds Industries advertising slogan, 1946

Once you are in this state, your mind is open to suggestion, and a skilled hypnotist will plant subtle counter-triggers in your mind to ward off your desire for cigarettes. It can also help to generally relax you and bring down your stress levels.

Once again, the knack is finding the right practitioner for you.

YOU CAN DO IT STANDING ON YOUR HEAD

Yoga in itself is not a direct method for giving up smoking, but it can prove to be a very useful ally. It's not a 'go-for-the-burn' physical activity and certain forms of it (Iyengar yoga is a good example) are very gentle indeed; you simply go with what you feel is comfortable.

What yoga can offer is a method of increasing the flow of endorphins through the body (the so-called 'natural happy drug'), creating a deep sense of well-being, which is both relaxing and energising. It's rather like creating a still pool in your life, and once you have learned a few positions it can be practised any time. Many leisure centres have yoga classes.

Similar claims could be made for meditation, which focuses on breathing. It's a great alternative to a smoke and gives you a natural high. Both yoga and meditation are relatively low cost options.

TAKE YOUR PICK

It's worth sampling a range of these alternative therapies and seeing what kind of mix works for you. From crystal healing to Bach Flower Remedies, from herbal remedies to primal scream, there could just be the method out there that will help you give up cigarettes. So check out your nearest complementary medicine centre, or even ask your doctor for what's available in your neighbourhood.

Don't think it won't ever happen to you. To find if your days are numbered you can count on IDEA 27, *Do you feel lucky, punk?*, to set you straight.

Try another idea...

'More than 34 million working days are lost each year because of smoking-related sick leave.'
www.patient.co.uk

Defining idea...

105

How did it go?

Q   All this new age stuff is just a pile of dingo's kidneys. It doesn't really work, does it?

A   *Don't knock it till you've tried it. When steam locomotives were first invented some people said that travelling at more than 25 mph would be fatal, that people's brains would explode. Ask drivers on any main road at rush hour and they'll tell you the opposite – it's travelling under that speed that's the problem. There's progress for you. Seriously, there's tens of thousands of people for whom these therapies have worked – you've just got to find the right one for you.*

Q   Why should I pay my hard-earned cash on a half chance that something might work when I can't afford it?

A   *You've no problem dishing out for a pack of your favourite drug though, have you? And that's guaranteed to kill you in the end. If you can't afford expensive therapists, check out your local library for a book on the subject. Most local authorities will also have information about very cheap courses – again, your local library is the best place to ask.*

Q   Would smoking herbal cigarettes be a good alternative?

A   *It really depends on whether you like smoking the equivalent of a garden hedge or not. You don't get the nicotine hit of a cigarette, just the sensation of setting fire to a bunch of leaves and sucking it into your lungs. Not recommended for most of us, but do try it out and let us know how you get on.*

23

First of the day

Every day when you wake up, cigarettes are clamouring at the front of queue, crying: FEED ME, BABY! FEED ME! You want it simple? This is it: never smoke your first cigarette of the day again and you've stopped forever.

There is a theory that smoking cigarettes is not a habit, it's a series of habits. We don't simply smoke cigarettes arbitrarily. Each one has a trigger, a link to some action or routine.

Let's take a look at the different kinds of cigarettes we smoke during the day and give them names. That way, we can pick them off one by one. Know your enemy, divide and conquer.

NAMING NAMES

First of the day

For most of us, the first cigarette of the day is our favourite, the one which gives us the most pleasure. Nicotine levels are low after a night's sleep so the hit is all the sweeter. Many of us will smoke a cigarette almost before we do anything else with our day. It could be with a cup of tea or coffee, almost certainly before breakfast and sometimes instead of it. A tricky one to give up.

Here's an idea for you...

Keep a log of all the cigarettes you smoke in a week. Note what time you light up and what event/opportunity it's connected to. Recognising the problem is the first step to curing it.

On the way to work

We need to sharpen our concentration, prepare ourselves for the tasks ahead (plus we know we may not get a cigarette break for another hour or two). Answer: light up a cigarette. But does it really sharpen our mind (and for how long?) or is that just an illusion the Tobacco Demon has planted?

Break time

The external discipline of a workplace is great for us as smokers: we're not allowed to smoke. The moment we can, we do; not necessarily because we want to, simply because it's permitted. And, of course, there's the cup of coffee – it has to be accompanied by a cigarette or it's just not the same. This cigarette relaxes and stimulates. Really?

The reward

The job's done (often with one or two cigarettes to help us focus on the work in hand) and we want to stand back and congratulate ourselves. We don't get a certificate or a silver cup, so we reward ourselves with a cigarette.

Try another idea...

Identify the enemy and knock 'em dead one by one. Try IDEA 26, *Slave to the weed*.

The stress reliever

Bad news, worry or just a bit of general stress. Poor us. Let's have a cigarette to calm our nerves, soothe ourself.

Phone call

We're like Pavlov's dogs. A little bell goes off and we salivate, or in our case we reach for the cigarettes and lighter.

After a meal

We've eaten well and we relax. Our defences are down and we take our eye off the ball for a second. Next thing we know we have a lit cigarette in our hand.

Work's over

The release of pressure means we celebrate our freedom, sending a signal to our deeply embedded habit that says: smoke a cigarette. Like with the coffee break, we also smoke simply because it's permitted.

With a drink

We're enjoying a leisurely drink, relaxing with friends or at home. Our ingrained pattern of behaviour automatically clicks in and triggers one 'pleasure' to go with another.

Last of the day

The day is done, time to wind down before bed. What better relaxant than a cigarette? Actually, there are hundreds, but reaching for a cigarette is easy and gives an instant (if momentary) satisfaction, which is why the last of the day often turns into two or even three.

Don't be tempted to think that some cigarettes are less dangerous than others. Try out IDEA 51, *One can't hurt.*

Try another idea...

'I like you more than I would like to have a cigarette.'
WENDY COPE, *Giving Up Smoking*

Defining idea...

'For most people smoking is a habit rather than an addiction. It is a ritual. It is a collection of thoughts, sensations, movements, actions, which all come together and centre on the lighting and smoking of a cigarette.'
MIRIAM STOPPARD, *Quit Smoking*

Defining idea...

There will be lots of other specific habitual cigarettes you'll be able to identify as you begin to analyse your personal smoker's profile. Tackle them one by one – corner the enemy in its favourite lair, then go for the jugular.

How did it go?

Q   I've identified all my regular cigarette habits, but I still find myself lighting up without thinking. How do I tackle this?

A   *Concentrate! The problem most of us have with smoking is that it has become such an ingrained habit that we do it without thinking. Like when we find we've lit two cigarettes because we've forgotten we started the first one. The crucial thing is to focus on our habit, bring it to the front of our consciousness, and be aware that we have a choice every time our little smoking demon prompts us: do we smoke this one or not?*

Q   I've cut down an awful lot, but I still find certain cigarettes are proving to be killers to overcome. How can I stop completely?

A   *It's that Tobacco Demon again, fighting a rearguard action. It knows you've decided to quit and you've got it worried. Knowing you're determined, it's playing the compromise game – it allows you to cut out the easy ones but digs in on a few key ones and defends them to the death (yours). Tackle them one at a time and direct all your energy at that one cigarette habit. Win that battle, then move on to the next. Trench warfare, a yard at a time. But be certain – you're bound to win in the end, because you're stronger than it is.*

24

Smokes and ladders

Some people stop and start again over the years. Although they have times when they don't smoke, at heart they still feel like smokers.

If this sounds familiar, there's no need to panic. Maybe you feel it would take a miracle to stop you smoking, but it just requires the right approach.

Let's imagine that tomorrow turns out to be the day you give up smoking for good. How will you know that things are going so well? What will you be doing differently that will indicate that something has happened this time that hasn't happened before?

We'd like you to imagine a day in the future when you are an ex-smoker. If you are not smoking, what will you be spending your time on instead? If you're not having to cough up for the cigarettes, how will you use the extra money? If you resist the urge to light up after dinner, what will you do with the additional time?

Now imagine a ladder with ten rungs. The tenth top rung represents your life as an ex-smoker and the bottom or first rung is the opposite: chain smoking all day and

Here's an idea for you...

Design your own bespoke smokes and ladders board. Make a zig-zag numbered path from the bottom of the board to the top. In ascending order, grade all the stages between being a confirmed smoker at the bottom and ex-smoker on the top. Include a few snakes (or smokes) for occasional relapses.

getting up several times at night to smoke. Where do you place yourself on this ladder? It is likely that you are somewhere in between, neither rock bottom nor near the top. The mere fact that you haven't got a foot on the floor is grounds for hope: it suggests that there are times that you are coping without smoking. There are times you persevere and are determined.

Take a few minutes to jot down what has helped you rise from the bottom rung to your present one and what stops you descending, especially in times of stress. This is the secret of your success and using it consciously could be the key to cracking the smoking habit. Now ask yourself what will tell you when you have moved up a rung or two. And finally, ask yourself how you will know when you have reached the top of the ladder.

Defining idea...

'To cease smoking is the easiest thing I ever did. I ought to know because I've done it a thousand times.'
MARK TWAIN (attributed)

When you've worked your way through this, you'll have a list of your strengths, skills and abilities as an ex-smoker. If you keep repeating the exercise at intervals, you'll be enjoying the view from the top before you even know it.

JACK'S LADDER

Jack started smoking behind the bike sheds as a 14-year-old schoolboy. He's 47 now, and not smoking quite as many as the sixty a day he consumed when his wife walked out on him, but on a bad day he can still burn through three packs. He lights up first thing in the morning, before and after meals, last thing at night and even if he gets up to relieve himself in the wee hours. Jack puts himself on the first rung of the ladder, as he knows he has been lower. He sees the next rung up as smoking only forty a day, the rung after that a mere thirty. Thereafter there would be longer and longer intervals between smokes, and delaying the first of the day till mid-morning.

JILL'S LADDER

Jill, 23, considers herself a social smoker. She only smokes when she goes out or feels really stressed out. Her gran died recently of a smoking-related disease and Jill has decided to give up altogether before the habit has got a firm hold of her. Currently she places herself on rung number seven and considers that she could rise to the next level if she were able to stand outside work with her mates without lighting up. The rung after that would be reached if she were able to spend a night in a pub or party without smoking, and rung ten would be not having smoked for six months and not missing it for three.

If using your imagination in a positive way helps you might also benefit from IDEA 6, *Imagine*, where you will find negative reinforcers.

Try another idea...

'I'm not really a heavy smoker any more. I only get through two lighters a day now.'
BILL HICKS, American comedian

Defining idea...

Q **I've managed to work up the ladder to rung seven and got stuck because I can't resist having one last cigarette at night. I've stopped everywhere else but just can't mange to stop myself then. What do you suggest?**

A *We think you ought to pat yourself on the back for getting this far. Why not try reminding yourself how you now only need one cigarette a day rather than twenty that you used to? Clearly you are doing something right. Giving up for good can take time, but you're heading in the right direction. You might also ask yourself, 'If I wasn't having a cigarette at the end of the day, what would I be doing?'*

Q **I smoke all day and half the night. You talk about a ladder, but I can only just make the floor. Can you help?**

A *Yes. Despite feeling stuck and hopeless, you're reading this and thinking about giving up, which is a start. Make a list of the sorts of things that would encourage you to become an ex-smoker and identify one small achievable step that could move you off the floor. There is only one direction for you to go in, and it's not down. Good luck.*

25

Words on paper

Keep a record of your struggle to give up. It will keep you on track and provide you with a document that you can be proud of.

No one to confide in? Fed up whinging to family and friends? Here's how to get problems off your chest without using others.

If you already record your private thoughts and feelings in a diary you won't need us to convince you about the many virtues of this sort of record keeping, nor the therapy and release it provides. But most of us don't keep a diary, perhaps considering it something to be left to narcissists and navel gazers. Keeping a written record, especially when going through a period of change, has a great deal going for it. Giving up smoking is a life-changing event, and the account of your campaign, your thoughts and feelings deserves to be secured to a page, even if you will be the only person who sees it.

WHY WRITING HELPS

Putting pen to paper or fingers to a keyboard provides an opportunity to reflect and process what is happening to you. Sometimes in the course of writing down a difficulty a solution will emerge from somewhere inside. More often, however, while describing, for example, your fear that you will surrender to the urge to 'just

Here's an idea for you... **Even if you are still smoking, start a diary today. Record your hopes and fears, anticipated difficulties and anything else related to smoking or giving up. Invest in a ring binder and paper or create a folder on your computer, whatever suits you best.**

have one', that anxiety may be replaced by resolve and the strength to carry on.

Used effectively, diaries are supporters and collaborators in the struggle against smoking. Keep one for a couple of weeks and you'll start to notice patterns. Some times of the week you'll manage to go without smoking for hours or even days. Once you've pinpointed them, doing more of whatever it is you do at those times is a great way of staying stopped for longer. Of course, keeping a tally of smoked cigarettes can be frightening when you realise just how many you have got through, but this doesn't have to be a bad thing. At least you'll know what you're up against and what you need to work on. Over the months, your diary will be a great gauge of how your quitting is progressing, and you'll be able to use it to track your recovery and predict what you need to do to get through those times of temptation.

Defining idea... *'I always say, keep a diary and some day it'll keep you.'*
MAE WEST

The most famous diarists developed a knack of using their diary like a dependable friend. Ann Frank, the Dutch Jewish girl in hiding during the Second World War, used to talk to hers like it was a sister or a pen pal, providing it with snippets of conversations or how she was improving her bedroom. Samuel Pepys, Kenneth Williams, Alan Clark – even Leo Tolstoy – used theirs to muse about their flawed personalities as well as record their thoughts on the events of the day.

A diary, in short, is always there to listen and, unlike other people, will never interrupt, disapprove or spit on your aspirations.

A NOTE ON NOTE KEEPING

Doctors and other professionals, like lawyers and accountants, keep notes on their patients or clients for good reason. Apart from monitoring progress, it provides the raw material and a memory aid that can be trawled for all sorts of easily forgotten details needed if they are unexpectedly required to write a report. You can take a leaf out of your doctor's book by keeping notes on your progress from smoker to ex-smoker. But, unlike your family doctor, you have plenty of time to spend with the patient and better access. Record your symptoms as honestly as possible: physical cravings, changes in mood, effect on your close relationships and anything you consider relevant. Unless you have neat handwriting, it might be worth typing these notes up, as they should make an excellent reference source and, should the worst happen and you do relapse, they will provide evidence that you can learn from.

Happy recording your thoughts but would like to join a group to share them? Turn to IDEA 32, *Strength in numbers*, for our thoughts on quit smoking support groups.

Try another idea...

GO PUBLIC

Another reason for making a record is that it gives you loads of free material that can be plundered, reshaped and flogged as newspaper copy. Why should anyone else, you might be asking, be interested in me giving up the weed? The answer is in the telling. Readers relate to a journalist who strikes a chord that resonates with their life or concerns. Smoking touches most people's lives one way or another. Rooting for you in your struggle to stop or hoping you'll fail should keep readers riveted. And if you crack the code and find the perfect way to quit, like Allen Carr you could write a series of books and become a multimillionaire.

'I never travel without my diary. One should always have something sensational to read on the train.'
OSCAR WILDE, *The Importance of Being Ernest*

Defining idea...

How did it go?

Q **I like the idea of keeping a diary as I quite like writing, but if past experience is anything to go on, it will peter out after about ten days. What do you learned hacks suggest?**

A *Have you considered writing notes with a view to using them as the raw material for a newspaper or magazine article? There are lots of people out there who'd like to give up, or at least read about someone in the throes of giving it a go. You might not get interest from one of the nationals, but there are hundreds of local newspapers and magazines that would be delighted to gobble up this sort of copy.*

Q **I've avoided writing all my life. It was one of the reasons I left school when I did. Just the thought of it brings back unhappy memories of English lessons and homework covered in red ink. This hasn't been a handicap in business, where I've managed pretty well. What do you suggest?**

A *Some English teachers really did more harm than good. Judging by your headed paper, your experiences at school have not held you back. Maybe you could keep an audio diary and get your secretary to type it up for you later. Alternatively, you could invest in some speech-recognition software, such as Dragon NaturallySpeaking, which will enable you to input into your PC without your secretary having to learn your innermost secrets.*

26

Slave to the weed

Let's face it – we are drug addicts. But nicotine, like many other drugs, is not a simple habit to crack. It's a collection of habits, triggered by certain events or actions in our day, each with its own battle to face.

Familiar patterns of behaviour are the smoke signals for our smoking demon who presses the button which triggers the reflex action to reach for the cigarette. Change the patterns, confuse the enemy and knock 'em dead one by one.

First of the day
Note the order you do things in first thing in the morning. Change it. What do you have for breakfast? Change it. So, if your normal routine is dress, coffee and cigarette, then off to work – change to orange juice with the newspaper, then dress; or if it's cigarette, then tea and toast – change to listen to the radio over your cup of tea, and buy yourself some tasty jam or marmalade to jazz up your toast. Change the routine, disrupt the ritual triggers.

It has been said that if you smoke twenty a day but only start at midday you stand a better chance of stopping than someone who only smokes ten a day but lights up first thing.

Here's an idea for you... **If you can't give up all at once (cold turkey), delay that first cigarette of the day. Build up in blocks of 10 or 15 minutes each day.**

On the way to work

If you drive, make a rule: no smoking in the car. Listen to the radio or take a music or talking book tape to listen to. If you live close to work, cycle or walk, remember not to take your cigarettes with you. If you take the bus or the train, take a newspaper or good novel and bury yourself in that. Make a rule: no smoking on the platform or in the bus queue.

Break time

Don't go outside with the smokers, follow the non-smokers' option. Change your drink if tea or coffee triggers the cigarette habit. Read your book, listen to music, find something practical to do with your hands.

Here's an idea for you... **Decide to stop – just like that. Don't smoke that last cigarette. Frame it in a sealed glass box and mount it somewhere prominent in the house.**

The reward

Give yourself a drink or a snack. Decide on something pleasurable to buy yourself that doesn't involve tobacco and fire. Close your eyes and dream of your next holiday, or any other satisfying images. Make a phone call, take a stroll.

The stress reliever

Using techniques like yoga, meditation or visualisation is a much more effective way of relieving or at least managing stress. Ideally you should find a relaxing position for any of these techniques, but meditation exercises can be done almost anywhere – there will almost certainly be local classes available to teach you the basics.

Phone call

Don't have your cigarettes, lighter or an ashtray near the phone. Instead, make sure you have a pad and pen to doodle with. Answer the phone with the opposite hand to the one you usually use. If it's relevant, use your free hand to pick up a document.

After a meal

If at home, make the dining room a non-smoking zone. Enjoy a new drink after the meal as your pleasurable reward. If in a restaurant or cafe, ensure the table you have chosen is in a non-smoking area, and resist the temptation to go and stand out in the rain.

Work's over

Once again, change your routine, do something different. Go shopping, pick up some brochures for your next holiday, avoid going for a drink with colleagues, change your route home, think about the evening ahead, plan tomorrow – do anything different to distract your mind from its all-too-familiar paths.

With a drink

Choose a non-smoking pub or part of the bar, eat peanuts, play on the games machine, select some of your favourite music on the jukebox, sit outside and enjoy the wildlife, play cards, do a pub quiz and concentrate on the questions. Above all, try and choose non-smokers to drink with, and if you can't, don't be tempted into accepting a cigarette.

Look how you can brighten up your own personal environment by kicking the weed in IDEA 35, Ashes to ashes.

Try another idea...

'Now the only thing I miss about sex is the cigarette afterward. Next to the first one in the morning, it's the best one of all. It tasted so good that even if I had been frigid I would have pretended otherwise just to be able to smoke it.'
FLORENCE KING

Defining idea...

'Coffee and tobacco are complete repose.'
Turkish proverb

Defining idea...

121

Last of the day

Distract yourself. Have a list of urgent jobs that need to be done around the home (we all have those), play with the children, take up a new hobby (particularly one that uses the hands). Set yourself an amount of time to do these activities in and the chances are you'll have passed the critical moment of the urge to smoke.

How did it go?

Q   I enjoy going to the pub with my mates for a drink. The trouble is, they all smoke, and it feels unnatural not to join in, doesn't it?

A   *The government may well lend a hand here. They've already done it in some countries like Ireland by banning smoking in public places. Lots of people still drink in Irish pubs but they don't smoke there any more. In the meantime, consider this – will your friends shun you forever if you choose not to smoke (and if they do, what kind of friends are they?)? And do you really want to be a victim of passive smoking without the rewards of smoking yourself?*

Q   I have a very stressful job. My main reason for smoking is to chill out and restore a sense of calm. If I don't smoke I get really strung out and on edge. After work I use cigarettes to relax. If I didn't I'd make my partner's life hell – and she isn't going to put up with that. And why should she?

A   *There are thousands of healthier ways to relieve stress and relax than smoking. Cigarettes are such a short-term fix and very inefficient. Try out some alternatives, whether it's yoga, long walks, worry beads, essential oils for a soothing bath. In fact, give them all a test drive until you find the ones that work for you.*

27

Do you feel lucky, punk?

Time for a squint at the statistics. We know that smoking's a risky business, but just how does it compare to other life-threatening activities? And how many of them would you volunteer for?

I once went on a school trip to a seaside resort. We had two hours of free time before attacking the fairground attractions in the afternoon. I wandered into an amusement arcade and, spurred on by an early win, gambled away my last penny. I spent the afternoon watching my schoolfriends having fun. I never gambled again.

ODDS ON

Despite this salutary childhood lesson, I never really learned. Although I can easily withstand the temptations of the lottery – there's more chance of dying by falling out of bed in Norfolk than hitting the jackpot – I gamble with my life every day.

Here's an idea for you...

Explore the internet. Type into your search engine words like 'tobacco-related diseases', 'emphysema', 'lung cancer'. Download and read at your leisure.

Now there are lies, damned lies and statistics, but we all use them in assessing life's risks. I know that if I drive through an amber traffic light, I'm increasing my chances of dying in a car crash, and that it's even more risky to drive home from the pub after six pints of Old Scrotum or eight Bacardi and Cokes.

Let's take a group of 1,000 average 20-year-old smokers and see what life holds in store for them. Of these:

- 1 will be a victim of murder or violent assault;
- 2 will end up serving jail sentences;
- 6 will die in car accidents;
- 250 will die from smoking-related diseases between 35 and 69;
- 250 will die from smoking-related diseases in old age.

You don't have to be a seasoned gambler to see the odds are heavily stacked against the smokers. In effect, if you smoke, you have a one in two chance of dying from it. You may not die young (one in four risk), but you will die horribly, unable to breathe, in agony or because your heart gives out.

So you have to ask yourself, do you feel lucky today, punk?

DEATH-DEFYING FEATS

Like estate agents, insurance companies are not our favourite people. They take our money and don't appear to do a lot for it. We pay our premiums and they run laughing all the way to the bank.

Our premiums are a gamble, both for us and for them. If we take out house insurance and nothing disastrous ever happens, the insurance company pockets all the cash, thanks very much. If the house is destroyed, the company coughs up and we get a good return on our payments. (Unless, of course, you haven't read subsection 87, clause 903 in the small print, in which you get zilch and have to live in a paper bag by the side of the road forever.)

Take a look at who benefits most from you continuing to smoke in IDEA 12, *Tobacco giants*.

Try another idea...

Insurance companies are not daft. Their job is to make money by taking the (safe) risk that enough of us won't die early enough to be able to rake in all the profits from a claim. They calculate the risk of us dying and set a premium that will mean overall they will always stash the cash. If there was no profit in it they wouldn't be doing it, they'd all become wheel clampers or solicitors.

'It's now proved beyond doubt that smoking is one of the leading causes of statistics.'
FLETCHER KNABEL, American journalist and writer

Defining idea...

TO DIE FOR

Take you as a smoker. What are the chances of you going to the great ashtray in the sky in the next ten years compared with other risky activities?

Have no fear of flying. Your chance of coming down in flames without a parachute is only 1 in 10,000,000. That's an awful lot of holidays in the sun before your number's up. If you live in California they reckon that even earthquakes give you the fairly decent odds of only a 1 in 60,000 chance of suffering premature burial.

Defining idea...

Leukaemia kicks in at 1 in 1250, and because of the nature of the disease the likelihood decreases as you get older. Unless, allegedly, you happen to live next to a nuclear power station or directly under electric power lines.

The open road gets a bit scarier. Car accidents lurch down to a somewhat unnerving 1 in 600. And whatever you do, don't get on a motorbike. On the back of one of those your chances slump to 1 in 50 (probably enhanced by all those lunatic car drivers).

Then we come to cigarette smokers, predictably high on the list. If you smoke a pack a day, insurers give you a 1 in 25 chance of dying in the next ten years. And this increases the longer you've smoked and the older you get.

That's why smokers get hammered by insurance companies. It's odds on you're going to be snuffed out sooner rather than later.

DEAD END

People die every day. Most from disease or accident, but some of us apparently through choice. Suicide by smoking is top of the class. Every year in the UK there are 2,000 deaths from infectious diseases, 3,000 from cirrhosis of the liver, 4,000 from actual suicide and 4,000 from road accidents.

Top of the heap though are the smokers. Around 120,000 of us go up in smoke each year (30,000 of those from lung cancer, 17,000 from heart disease).

So weigh up the odds. If you stop smoking before 35 your life expectancy is only slightly less than people who've never smoked. If you stop before 50 your risk drops by half. And it's never too late to stop. You'll almost definitely live longer. Racing certainty.

Q   My mum always said that you had more chance of dying by being run over by a bus than from smoking. She's right, isn't she?

How did it go?

A   *It's difficult facing up to the fact that a parent has lied to you, or is not in fact infallible, but go back and look at the statistics above. And answer these questions – was your mum a smoker (or did she live with one)? How old was she when she died? Most importantly, did she get run over a by a bus or die from a smoking-related disease?*

Q   I'm going to die anyway. I live in a car-crazy big city and work in a dirty industry. That will probably kill me on its own. What the heck, I'll smoke, too. Who cares which one gets me first?

A   *Don't you like living? If you contract a smoking-related illness, you certainly won't like dying. You should do everything you can to reduce your chances of dying horribly. You may not be able to change your job or where you live, but smoking is one risk you can choose not to take.*

28

No respecter of reputations

Prince or pauper, millionaire or milkman, smoking ruthlessly slays its users.

Apart from having a few bob more than the rest of us, what have King George VI of England, Louis Armstrong, Jackie Kennedy and Bob Marley got in common? Death from a smoking-related illness.

Smoking is such a widely practised habit that it's easy to ignore just how lethal long-term use can be. It has been estimated that half of all long-term smokers will die of a smoking-related illness. One way of bringing home this message is considering the effect cigarettes have had on people you have heard of, people in the public eye.

DEATHWATCH

There are websites that list the names of famous people who have died of a smoking-related condition. One long list is full of personalities from all parts of show business and public life. Louis Armstrong from the world of jazz, Lucille Ball and Jack Benny some will remember from childhood telly, Gary Cooper, Clark Gable, Steve McQueen from Hollywood, Ian Fleming, F. Scott Fitzgerald and Dashiel

Here's an idea for you... **Overexposure to government health warnings can make you immune to them. Compensate for this by making up your own health warnings based on smoking-related illnesses that run in your family or those your icons have succumbed to.**

Keep a scrapbook of newspaper and magazine clippings about well-known people reported to be suffering from the first serious signs of a smoking-related illness or disease. Group the people into categories like film, literature, television and royalty, and plot their progress. Next time you feel like lighting up, take ten minutes to look through your clippings.

Hammett batting for the writers, Princess Margaret representing the royals and so on and on. If all the people on this list had been killed in road or air accidents, there's a fair chance that flying and motoring would have been made safer. But they weren't and the grim reaper continues to pull in smokers early, sometimes decades early, with monotonous regularity.

What makes lists like this extra depressing is that on the whole everyone who is featured on them was mega-rich; they were able to afford the best medical advice, treatment and care, yet nothing they could buy made a jot of difference in the end. Good terminal medical and nursing care is no replacement for a healthy old age.

Knowing the plight of so many rich and famous smokers is of itself unlikely to stop you smoking. However, the gradual build up of this knowledge can add to your resolve, especially when it's allied to other strategies. Here are a few ways of doing this.

MAKE YOUR OWN LOCAL LIST

Compile lists of famous British, Scottish, Irish, Canadian or Aussie victims of smoking. Or be even more specific and restrict your search to, say, Oxford, New

York, Sydney or Paris. You could start by, say, plundering the American site for Brits: George Harrison, Edward VIII and Noel Coward. Then, rather than just leaving it as a simple list, find out more about each subject. What specifically did they die of? How old were they? And were they moderate or serious smokers? You could research further by checking out medical books what would happen to you if, like Sigmund 'A cigar is also a cigar' Freud, you develop jaw cancer.

FAMILY TREES

If, quite frankly, you find that celebrities just don't do it for you– not even dead ones – you may wish to branch out in another direction and consider the people in your own extended family whose lives were terminated due to smoking the leaves of the tobacco plant. Your granddad might have had an eighty-a-day habit well into his hundredth year, but tracking down your ancestors and their fates could show you that great uncles Arthur and Herbert weren't so lucky. This is certainly worth finding out, as studies have shown that there are hereditary predispositions to many smoking-related illnesses. So if a number of your kith and kin have surrendered to a particular cancer, heart or circulation problem, you will be more vulnerable than most.

Try another idea...

Like to read something about the ageing effects of smoking? Brace yourself and turn to IDEA 11, *The shock of the old.*

Defining idea...

'On CBS Radio the news of Ed Murrow's death, reportedly from lung cancer, was followed by a cigarette commercial.'
ALEXANDER KENDRICK

Defining idea...

'I don't want to achieve immortality through my work... I want to achieve it through not dying.'
WOODY ALLEN

How did it go?

Q **I still don't understand how knowing that all these famous people died of cancer or something will help me to give up. Would you explain it, please?**

A *Many of the people cited here have become role models to millions through exposure in the media, and their behaviour is copied everywhere. Most of them made no secret of their smoking habit and in doing so inadvertently stamped their seal of approval on it. In itself, this knowledge is unlikely to stop you smoking, but, coupled with other factors like noticing adverse health symptoms and how much the habit is hurting your pocket, it should have a sobering effect.*

Q **I love classic films and Humphrey Bogart is one of my favourite stars. Why are you tarnishing his reputation?**

A *When someone is given iconic status fans invest them with superhuman qualities. The actor John Wayne, for instance, would get mixed up with the superheroes he played on screen. All we are pointing out is that these people are made of the same stuff as the rest of us and are just as vulnerable to the lethal effects of smoking. This is not an indictment of Bogart's ability to act or a reflection of the sort of human being he was.*

29

The sweet smell of success

Sometimes stopping smoking seems impossible. It's time to remind you that there are smokers out there who have stopped.

We know that giving up is hard to do, but people are doing it everywhere.

You can get so depressed about the information you discover in newspapers, books and magazines about the havoc that smoking is doing to your health, your relationships and your pocket that you might be tempted to give up reading. Before you do, however, spare a few minutes while we trawl through our successful quitters file and revisit a pair of the case histories of people we know who have put the smoking habit behind them.

PAULINE

Pauline is Clive's wife. Fifteen years ago she was living and working in Italy. She never smoked before noon, but between then and the time she went to bed she got through 15–20 cigarettes. In Italy at that time women didn't smoke in public, perhaps they still don't, so when she was working in a shop she would have to nip out the back for a furtive quick one. She was struck down by a respiratory condition which made her bed-bound for three days. During this period she was unable to smoke, and when she felt better she said to herself 'I've got through that, I don't

Here's an idea for you...

Ex-smokers are everywhere – people who were once as hooked as you are now. Talk to non-smoking friends and colleagues and you'll discover that many of them were once moderate or even heavy smokers. Ask them how and why they stopped, whether they still get the odd craving and what they do about it, and what advice they would give to someone contemplating giving up. Learn from their experience.

need to smoke anymore.' And she hasn't. This isn't quite true. Once, when her son broke his arm, someone thrust a cigarette in her direction and she gratefully accepted it, but that was that. Very, very occasionally she sees a group smoking outside socially and joins them, but this is rare. She considers herself a non-smoker and isn't tempted back into the fold, even though she spends a considerable amount of time working in prisons – an institution dominated by a smoking culture that affects prisoners and staff alike. She recalls how she felt having given up all those years ago: 'It was a feeling of relief.'

ARVID

Arvid is one of Peter's brothers. He started smoking back in the early seventies while a 19-year-old bandsman in the British Army. Cheap cigarettes were one of the few perks that came with the job, there wasn't really anything else. In the three decades since, Arvid estimates that he has tried to give up at least twenty times. Arvid decided to stop on this occasion because he was tired of the coughing, the breathlessness and other impacts on his health. He recently finished his second course of the smoking cessation drug Zyban. He first tried it six years ago, but got frightened off by an article in a newspaper which suggested that

Defining idea...

'Sometimes a cigar is just a cigar.'
SIGMUND FREUD

people who took this medication were dropping like flies. But this time he wasn't put off by Zyban scare stories. The drug worked, and after twelve weeks he was down to a single tablet every five days. Since finishing the course he hasn't restarted smoking.

If you would like to read about the process of giving up and how far you've yet to go, turn to IDEA 5, *The seven stages of man giving up*.

Try another idea…

During past attempts, giving up made him bad tempered and irritable, and even staunch non-smoker friends and family would plead with him to restart. But this wasn't the case this time. Arvid has also been gratified by the positive support he has received from other ex-smokers – many of them virtual strangers. People who are happy reliving the excitement and enthusiasm they felt when they were finally rid of this burden. A talented musician, Arvid has used the money he hasn't spent on cigarettes to buy himself two new guitars. Cigarettes were costing him £40 a week, so the money quickly added up.

'I didn't give up cigarettes, I was so ill I couldn't smoke. I just never started again.'
KEITH WATERHOUSE, journalist and novelist

Defining idea…

How did it go?

Q   **Being told about people who have successfully given up makes me feel worse. I've been trying to quit for years, then something comes up and I'm back to square one. Can you offer some hope?**

A   *Try not to be disheartened. This idea isn't about you comparing yourself unfavourably with successful ex-smokers and giving yourself a hard time for not being one of them yet. It's more like having an instant support group of inspiring folk who've been there and done it and are there to give you some tips just when you need them most.*

Q   **A lot of people I thought of as non-smokers light up after a few drinks. It seems like a tempting compromise, but how can I make sure I don't slip straight back into my old forty-a-day routine?**

A   *For most people who give up, it's easier to go from sixty a day to none ever again than from sixty a day to five a year. That said, there are a few ex-smokers who can morph back into smokers at parties. These party smokers all seem to have something in common: they've broken their old smoking rituals and found other ways to deal with most of their usual cigarette triggers. Some people manage this by switching to the odd cigar after special meals out or puffing on a pipe at Christmas. Either way, if your friends manage to be occasional party smokers and you're still chaining your way through the week, you could do a lot worse than to join them.*

30

Phone a friend

**Finding the right person to help you quit could be the
difference between success and failure.**

*A problem shared is a problem halved.
Giving up can be a lot easier if there is
someone available to share the load.*

Before putting their name forward in a leadership contest, politicians first nominate a
campaign manager. This custom is so widely accepted that no one would dream of
running for high office without one. For good reason: managers will keep prospective
candidates informed of problems ahead, keep them focused on the task, maintain
morale when setbacks occur and stop complacency creeping in when things are going
rather well. In short, they remain level-headed at times of stress and change. While
this is not an easy role to perform, it's much easier to do for someone else.

The problems faced by smokers trying to give up have certain similarities with those
encountered by someone running for office. (If only you could be voted in as a non-
smoker.) Their tried and tested solution, of getting a campaign manager, is one that
can be adapted to your own campaign. If you live in the UK you could refer yourself
to your nearest NHS quitline service. There are also private counsellors offering one-
to-one help and support for smokers. Many of these have merit, but they usually
come at a price and we reckon that it shouldn't be too difficult to find and nurture
your own cigarette cessation coach.

Here's an idea for you...

Before you phone a friend and ask for help in quitting, sit down and write a job spec. This will need to include what you expect from your friend as a coach, how they can help, whether you'll have prearranged meetings or you just need someone who'll respond to crisis.

FIND A FRIEND

The qualities needed to help someone give up smoking (or any other addiction) are many and varied. Indeed, the list is so long that it is nigh on impossible to find them all in the same person. But if you can find someone who really wants to help you quit, is patient, calm under pressure, can see the wood for the trees and can help you discover creative solutions, then you're onto a winner. We all know people who make us feel highly intelligent and better able to understand things in their presence, just as we can identify those who make us feel stupid and dumb. The knack is to home in on the first group: positive, empathic types who believe that anything is achievable and setbacks are only there to make life more interesting.

Why would this wonderful person want to help you? Their time is not infinite, after all, and there are lots of good causes out there competing for their time and energy. We suggest that you compile a list of strong reasons why quitting smoking will improve your life and that of the people around you: how it will improve your relationship with your partner, improve your fitness and therefore extend your sporting (and sexual) career, and make you a better role model for your kids. There must be a bunch of other examples you can think of. You'll also need to persuade them that giving up is going to be a really tough challenge for you and that their help will be vital to keep you on track when times get hard. You can specify the unique qualities they have and what you hope their role could be.

Defining idea...

'The cigarette is a portable therapist.'
TERRI GUILLEMENTS

Does your coach need to be an ex-smoker? Having someone who has successfully completed the process certainly helps, as they'll have first-hand experience of what you are going through and are living evidence that it can be done. On the other hand, all smokers

Not convinced that you want to put all your eggs in the one basket? Go to IDEA 32, *Strength in numbers*, and learn more about group support.

Try another idea...

are different and other qualities possessed by a lifelong non-smoker could outweigh their lack of experience. After all, you don't expect your doctor to have suffered from a particular bug before you go and consult her.

DRAWING UP A JOB SPEC

Job specifications, the sort your employer might or might not have given you (or expect you to produce yourself), tend not to be very useful. A paper exercise imposed by governments that has little to do with your day-to-day job and everything to do with ticking boxes. The job spec we have in mind attempts to be a useful document that helps both you and your cessation coach know what is expected from them: a summary, if you like, and a means to implement it. Review dates and ways of responding to relapses and crisis of confidence. It should recognise the time and effort involved, and outline ways the coach can be rewarded. This process might feel heavy handed and unnatural if dealing with an old mate, but its serious nature keeps the mind concentrated and makes the task feel achievable. This is the time to discuss potential problems and what can be learnt from previous attempts to give up. This approach is not a replacement for other methods of quitting, rather a means of supplementing them.

'I'm glad I don't have to explain to a man from Mars why each day I set fire to dozens of little pieces of paper, and put them in my mouth.'
MIGNON MCLAUGHLIN

Defining idea...

REWARDS

There are very few truly saintly people who do things for purely altruistic reasons. Money may be vulgar, but so is just saying thank you. You can't expect a friend to give you a reasonable charge for their time and effort, so you need to be ingenious in finding ways to reward your coach. In addition to acknowledging how much you appreciate their ongoing support, find out what they like – flowers, books, CDs, trips to the theatre – and make sure they accept them even if they say no at first.

How did it go?

Q   **There's one person I know who'd be great for this job but unfortunately he moved to Sydney 18 months ago. I really can't think of anyone else. What should I do?**

A   *There's no reason not to conduct the whole process by email. This form of communication has much to offer. You'll need to find words that can explain how you feel adequately and you'll need time to reflect on what your coach has written in reply.*

Q   **I found this wonderful man who's been helping me give up. When we go to a bar I always try to buy the drinks, but he insists on paying his own way; and he got quite annoyed when I bought him a present. He says he was helped to give up and this is his way of repaying his mentor. What should I do?**

A   *Tell your friend that you'll do the same for someone else once you have successfully given up. A few more people like him around and the tobacco trade would be rocked to its foundations.*

31

Shared air

You're never alone with a Strand, according to the ad from the 1950s. (The ad became a cult, the brand bombed.) There are almost always people around you when you smoke. What are we doing to them when we blow out our hot air?

Oxygen is good for you. The entire planet agrees on this. Your body can't function without it. But if you smoke, you may not be getting enough. So why aren't you taking your fair share of air?

There's been a lot of debate about whether inhaling someone else's smoke can be harmful, even if you're not a smoker yourself. Recent research has shown, however, that it's extremely dangerous. You are 20–30% more likely to suffer from heart disease and diseases of the blood vessels if you regularly breathe in other people's cigarette smoke. The risk of strokes rises by 80%.

PARTNERS IN GRIME

Those at most risk are the partners or children of smokers, particularly if you regularly smoke in the same room or car as them. They haven't decided to smoke, you've chosen for them.

Here's an idea for you...

Limit yourself to only smoking when you're absolutely alone and outside. Make a rule never to smoke in an enclosed space again. Buy a warm raincoat if it's winter, because you'll have to battle the elements as well as your addiction.

To see the danger, you only have to look at the number of people who have died from smoking-related diseases simply because they worked in a smoky workplace, like a pub or club. They're subjected to an atmosphere that is thick with the poisons from smoking and have no option but to breathe it in. Don't force it on them.

Tobacco smoke is also an irritant, and can make asthma and other breathing conditions worse. Nowhere is this shown more obviously than in children. If you have children you can make an immediate improvement in their health by choosing not to smoke in the same room as them.

Two out of three people now say that being in a smoky room bothers them. Smoke affects the eyes, nose and throat. It can lead to coughs, nausea, dizziness or headaches in non-smokers. So don't smoke in company.

Defining idea...

'An estimated 17,000 children in the UK under 5 are hospitalised each year for chest infections related to parents' smoking.'
GASP Smoke Free Solutions, 'Passive Smoking: The Facts' leaflet

Most of the smoke caused by a cigarette is released into the air. This is called sidestream smoke, and is just as deadly as the stuff you suck down into your lungs. And then you breathe out.

The tobacco smoke in a room is 85% sidestream, 15% exhaled mainstream smoke. Of the 4,700 chemicals released in cigarette smoke at least 60 are known to cause cancer. Indeed, sidestream smoke has higher concentrations of many of the cancer-inducing chemicals and toxins. Bet you didn't know that.

PREGNANT WITH MEANING

If you're sensible, as soon as you find out you're going to have a baby you'll stop smoking. But this counts for very little if your partner or other members of your family continue smoking around you. Tell them they're risking the health of your unborn child and ask them to be considerate.

Inhaling tobacco smoke reduces the amount of oxygen that is supplied to the baby through the placenta at a time when it's absolutely vital to its growth and well-being. If the mother is exposed to smoke there is an increased risk of miscarriage, and the baby is much more likely to be born early or with a low birth weight. These babies are more prone to illness and infections.

Would you be able to forgive yourself if your unborn child was damaged because of your selfish habit?

PROTECT AND SURVIVE

Even if you're a smoker you should acknowledge that your smoke can kill others. One day very soon, when you've given up smoking, you'll want to protect yourself against others' smoke, so, starting now, this is what you do.

You were young once. Shouldn't you be setting an example to the younger generation? Have a look at what tempted us in the first place in IDEA 8, *Superkings*?

Try another idea…

'Childhood asthma is more common and asthma attacks are more frequent and severe for children exposed to tobacco smoke. Up to 120,000 visits to the doctor for asthma every year are attributed to passive smoking.'
GASP Smoke Free Solutions, 'Passive Smoking: The Facts' leaflet

Defining idea…

At work insist that your employer introduces a smoke-free workplace policy, to protect your fellow workers from the smokers (especially if you're one yourself). In any public

143

space, such as restaurants, pubs and hotels, insist on a non-smoking area and complain if they don't have one. Never accept 'no'; if this is what they tell you, go elsewhere.

Most of all, at home, ban yourself from smoking indoors or in any other enclosed space you share with your children or partner.

How did it go?

Q   I'm thoroughly fed up of being made to feel guilty for smoking like I'm some kind of social pariah with a dreadful disease. Why should I feel bad?

A   Given that so few people smoke now, we're in a minority, Harry. And unfortunately we are social pariahs. And if we don't already have a dreadful disease, we probably will have – we just don't know which one yet. Unless you're one of those people who play their iPod at full volume with faulty headphones, you probably get very annoyed at those who do disturbing your peace, and why not? Non-smokers feel the same, only more so. There's no evidence yet to suggest that other people's loud personal stereos can kill you – but other people's smoke can.

Q   I'm desperate to stay off cigarettes but I really like going for a drink. It's impossible to escape smoky bars surely?

A   Impossible is a strong word. More and more public spaces, if not slapping a outright ban on all smoking, are providing smoke-free spaces. After all, not all drinkers smoke. Sounds like you'll just have to go on a pub crawl until you find one that gives you space to breathe. Then tempt all your friends there. Where there's a will...

32

Strength in numbers

Haven't got the willpower to go it alone? Joining a group could give you the extra resolve.

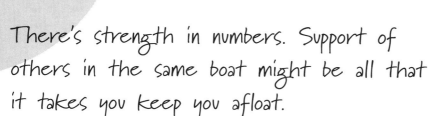

There's strength in numbers. Support of others in the same boat might be all that it takes you keep you afloat.

Groups work. They might not work for everyone, but there's convincing evidence that joining and attending a specialist support group can help people overcome serious addictions to alcohol, hard drugs and gambling. Support groups also work for people who are serious about giving up cigarettes. Quitting smoking on your own is a lonely and morale-sapping process: there's no one around to pat you on the back after that first smoke-free day. There's no one to confide in when your resolve starts to slip and you're wondering if it's all worth the hassle. And when you do crack and light up, there's no one around who's been there before to offer empathy or helpful strategies to get you back on track when you're full of remorse and self-loathing.

HOW GROUPS WORK

The first UK therapy groups were started by a number of army medical officers in World War Two. They decided to round up soldiers suffering from shell shock and treat them collectively, getting them to share experiences and support each other.

No smoking cessation groups in your area other than ones run by idiots? Set up your own. You'll probably have to do some reading or pick the brains of someone running another group. You may also need help setting it up, the use of a venue and places to advertise. Plaster details and a contact number in health centres and shop windows, and arrange a preliminary meeting.

The experiment was a success and when the war ended these pioneers applied the same techniques to civilians with a variety of psychiatric and social difficulties. AA – that's alcoholics anonymous, not the motoring organisation – dates back even further, to 1934, when a group of American reformed drinkers started meetings helping members live without booze one day at a time. Whether led by doctors (or other health professionals) or ex-addicts, the rationale is the same: a belief that problems are best tackled with the support and help of others.

Being a member of a team is likely to increase your resolve and commitment to any agreed task. Just think how hard members of a successful football team work for each other. Not wanting to let the side down is a strong motivator, and having other people in your group sharing your success and you sharing theirs can help you stick to the task in times of difficulty when, if left to your own devices, you might otherwise slacken. Groups where the focus is on overcoming a craving for nicotine will contain a cluster of individuals each with first-hand knowledge of being a smoker and each with their own insights into what does and doesn't work. When this empathy, energy, expertise and enthusiasm is pooled it's potent stuff. Non-smoking health professionals who have never given up cannot truly understand what it feels like to crave a cigarette in times of stress, but other members of the group certainly do. Some are able to put into words thoughts you feel but can't quite express, while someone else might

Defining idea...

'Smoking is pulmonary rape.'
Anon.

be able to identify with a problem you talk about and suggest a useful strategy that worked for them. By taking place at prearranged intervals, group meetings act as focal points: 'There's a meeting on Wednesday if I can just hang on' might just give you the

Group therapy not for you? Why not have a look at IDEA 30, *Phone a friend*, and consider the support you can get from one special person?

Try another idea...

extra impetus to keep saying no. The group can also be a place to bring and leave a mixture of feelings. A shared task with like-minded people all fighting a common enemy is likely to forge strong friendships. Another advantage of being in a group rather than being with an individual therapist is that group members can tell you things about yourself that a professional might be reluctant to say. It might be hard to hear, but it's helpful in the long run.

SO WHAT HAPPENS?

Whether you are a founder member of a new group or are joining an existing one such as one run by the NHS in the UK, you are likely to feel uncomfortable initially. You and other members are bound to be eyeing each other up and wondering whether you can trust each other. Men in particular seem to find it hard to talk about how they feel, their fear of failure, their need for the support of others and a whole raft of different niggles. Generally, if made welcome, most people settle down quickly and start to benefit from hearing other people's plights which are likely to resonate with their own. Joining a group of like-minded individuals who are determined to quit acts as a counterweight to internal and external pressures to light up and revert to the old ways again.

'The believing we do something when we do nothing is the first illusion of tobacco.'
RALPH WALDO EMERSON

Defining idea...

147

Good therapists have a knack of making new members feel welcome, ensuring that everyone is listened to and taken seriously, and are able to tactfully shut up people who want to hog the centre ground. It actually doesn't matter whether he or she has smoked or not, is young or old, gay or straight: good leaders can be any of these things and it is best to approach these meetings with an open mind. An ability to ensure fair play and keep everyone within agreed boundaries is what really matters.

How did it go?

Q **I'd like to join a group but I work shifts and don't think I'd be able to go regularly. I've tried joining evening classes in the past, but always had to drop out as I'd miss a few weeks and get behind in the course work. What do you suggest?**

A *You're right – most groups demand a commitment and expect you to be there most of the time. Perhaps you need to discuss this with colleagues and your boss and see if you can change shifts. You will, of course, have to pay the time and goodwill back to the people at work, but if it helps you manage to give up it will have been worthwhile.*

Q **I've got mixed feelings about joining a group. I've never been a therapy junkie and the thought of talking in front of a bunch of strangers freaks me out. Is it worth taking the plunge?**

A *Initially most people feel backward about coming forward. Established members and a good leader will help you find your feet. When you are giving up smoking it is a great idea to acquire a new skill, like talking in public, as it will improve your self-confidence.*

33

I want it now

Ever wondered why sound health and monetary reasons for quitting don't spur your stopping?

If you gave up now you could extend your life by years, be better off financially and have fewer wrinkles, so what's stopping you, ol' prune eyes?

Do you realise how much money you spend on cigarettes? It doesn't take more than a few minutes to work out on the back of a packet of twenty the thousands you hand over every year to your friendly tobacconist. Sensible people have been telling you to think of the cost since before you started. And have you thought about what you could get if you put all this money in a jar under your bed? A few years down the line you could be driving the car of your dreams, live in a better home, have holidays you now can only lust over or get a new, slightly higher bed to keep it all under. Feel free to add your own examples. The question is, why isn't this knowledge enough to stop you smoking? Indeed, the more sensible people tell you the benefits of stopping, the more it seems to make you want to continue. Why?

The short answer is they are on the wrong wavelength. They are mixing up long- and short-term gratification. A puff of a cigarette provides a nicotine rush that hits your brain within seven seconds. It also carries a hefty price tag (but no matter),

Here's an idea for you... **Work out how much you spend on cigarettes per day or week. Now price luxury items using these units. If a CD, say, costs three days' smoking, buy yourself one after three days; if it's a bottle of vintage champagne, buy one after a week. Make a wish list of luxuries that are currently out of your price range: that sports motorbike, designer suit, hot tub – the sky's the limit.**

these magical moments pass quickly (but they were good while they lasted) and the heady buzz is soon replaced by a craving for more (but you know what to do about that). Saving up for that beautiful sports car, on the other hand, takes years. It's pointless trying to replace short-term gratification with a long-term alternative. It just won't work: or will it?

You can get long-term gratification from giving up smoking, or anything else for that matter, but it takes time. The thing to do is get to your goal in a series of steps. The initial steps should be close together and relatively easy to achieve, then as you progress the distance between them should gradually increase. This principle is similar to that used by doctors helping someone to come off an addictive drug. In our case, as you will see from the suggestions below, you start by rewarding yourself with small treats on a daily basis for the first week and thereafter you give yourself bigger treats less often. Cigarettes, in the UK at least, are so expensive that you don't need to be a heavy smoker to soon build up a valuable DVD collection or expensive wardrobe. Not paying the government vast quantities of tax is an added bonus.

It doesn't matter what you do as long as you spend all the money you would have spent on cigarettes and you spend it on the days specified.

TOUGH LOVE

The hard bit is that you'll have to tell your partner and family that initially all the money you'll be saving from not smoking will have to be spent on luxuries for you, and you alone. If you're given a hard time, just blame us. After all, our shoulders are broad and our telephone numbers ex-directory. You could also point out that at least they won't be any worse off and might benefit indirectly by being with someone who smells sweetly of perfume rather than Marlboro or Benson & Hedges.

Here are our suggestions to help you spend your well-gotten gains.

Quitter's milestones
- Day 1: coffee and cake at a pavement café.
- Day 2: mini-manicure, or women to have more coffee and cake.
- Day 3: treat yourself to a new paperback.
- Day 4: browse in a record shop for a budget-price CD.
- Day 5: flowers.
- Day 6: trip to cinema.
- Day 7: perfume or aftershave.
- Day 10: quality haircut.
- Day 14: new item of clothing.
- Day 21: bottle of vintage wine.
- Day 28: take partner for an expensive celebratory meal.

Smoking is less popular than it once was. More and more people are managing to give up. Check out IDEA 36, *If you can't beat them, join them*, to help spur you on.

Try another idea...

'What a weird thing smoking is and I can't stop it. I feel cosy, have a sense of wellbeing when I'm smoking, poisoning myself, killing myself slowly. Not so slowly maybe. I have all kinds of pains I don't want to know about and I know that's where they're from. But when I don't smoke I scarcely feel as if I'm living. I don't feel I'm living unless I'm killing myself.'
RUSSELL HOBAN

Defining idea...

151

- Six weeks in: get teeth whitened.
- Twelve weeks in: go away for a luxury weekend.
- Six months in: day spa and full range of pampering and treatments or new mountain bike.
- One year after stopping: luxury holiday.

How did it go?

Q **Nice idea, but I'm using nicotine replacement patches and they're nearly as expensive as cigarettes. Perhaps in a month I'll be able to afford a thimbleful of coffee (no milk or sugar). What do you suggest?**

A *Umm, you've almost stumped us. In your case you'll need to be creative and find non-monetary ways of rewarding yourself – perhaps time treats, like quality time with the family or making an extra effort to go out and be entertained. Alternatively, work out how much you would spend on cigarettes in a year, subtract the cost of the course of NRT and spend the balance the way we have suggested. You'll have to scale down your rewards but you won't be fighting the same level of cravings as people giving up cold turkey. Luckily you shouldn't need to be taking patches for the rest of your life, so even you will be better off in the long run.*

Q **This idea appeals to me, but I can see myself getting a lot of grief from my partner when he realises you're telling me to spend all the money on myself. What do you suggest?**

A *Actually, if you enjoy it, there's no reason why you can't spend money on your partner. The key thing is that you get the reward for your own effort, but if your partner gains too, good for him.*

34

Helping your helpers help you

Want a mate to help you quit? Here are some suggestions for your chum to take on board.

Don't feel confident enough to give up smoking alone and think you know someone who will hold your hand during your troubled times ahead? Get them reading this idea.

MANY HANDS STOP LIGHTER WORKING

So you've been asked or have agreed to help a friend give up smoking. You might be wondering how you can do this, whether you are the right person to help or whether you'll just make things worse. Do you know how serious your quitter is about giving up? Will they buckle when the going gets tough or will they soldier on?

While you can't know for sure, initial groundwork should give you some idea of your friend's motivation, what it is they need, and whether you have the necessary time and desire to help them. Even if you have known your friend for years, we suggest that you still make a formal contract. Decide what both parties expect from the relationship, agree some basic rules and make contingency plans in case of

Here's an idea for you... **You've probably got lots of friends prepared to help you give up who don't know how to respond to a non-specific plea for help. So be particular? Ask them to text you once a week to catch up with how the quitting is going. If they normally buy duty-free tobacco for you when returning from holiday, give them a list of alternatives, like perfumes, aftershave or alcohol.**

relapses or other crises. This early meeting is crucial as it can prevent a great deal of misunderstanding later on. Prearranging review dates to monitor progress might remind you of work, but if tackled in the right spirit they can keep the project on track.

TAKE A SMOKER'S HISTORY

Even if you know your smoker well, it's still worth taking a formal history of their smoking habit. Prepare a crib sheet of questions, and make sure they are open ones, like: How did you start smoking? When did you become a regular user? What are all the different cigarettes you have each day? What will you miss about smoking? Where or when will you be most tempted to light up? What other problems do you anticipate? Have you have tried to give up before and, if so, what happened (other than that you failed)? Can you imagine being a non-smoker and, if so, what would that be like?

A FRIEND IN NEED

If you record the answers to these and any other observations that crop up you'll have a comprehensive knowledge of your friend as a smoker. Armed with this information, you are well placed to help identify the best ways of helping your friend to

Defining idea... **'Teamwork makes the impossible simple.'**
Anon.

quit. Some people need personal support – constant chivvying, cajoling or stroking; others need help with organising a strategy, or help in identifying things and places they should avoid to reduce temptation. If you have given up yourself, just being there and proving that it is possible should be a great help. While everyone copes differently while quitting, telling your friend how you felt when you were going through it should be of comfort: like a person walking ahead through a black tunnel shining a lamp and pointing out the hazards.

For more on this theme from a smoker's perspective see IDEA 30, *Phone a friend*.

Try another idea…

Good friends seem to have a knack of knowing what to do in different circumstances. They are there for the bad times as well as the good, they dampen down enthusiasm when you start getting a little too cocky and lackadaisical, and they boost your morale when you are feeling low. They seem to possess complementary knowledge and skills when our own stock is depleted and sometimes they just work wonders behind the scenes, sorting things out.

'Few things are harder to put up with than the annoyance of a good example.'
MARK TWAIN

Defining idea…

Q **I reluctantly agreed to help a mate give up. At first he was keen and everything went well. Recently he's been acting oddly towards me and even avoiding me. Although he says he's still not smoking, other friends have seen him having the occasional furtive puff. What should I do?**

A *Oh dear, these things happen. While it would be easy to suggest that you cut your losses and just walk away, now is the time he most needs help. Meet with him and put all your cards on the table. Tell him what you've heard and offer him either a fresh start or a chance to dissolve this relationship. What he does with his life is his decision, not yours, but you can help him make his choice.*

Q **I offered to help this person give up and now I wish I hadn't. I know how difficult it is to quit – I used to smoke up to fifty a day – but I can't believe the abuse I'm being subjected to. She always apologises afterwards, but I still feel hurt and upset. I'm only trying to help. Should I quit?**

A *It's dreadful to feel you're being used as a scapegoat like this. It's worth considering how professional therapists cope in these circumstances. In essence, they establish a set of ground rules early on, spelling out what they consider acceptable in the relationship and what they will do if that boundary is breached. They don't just do this for physical and verbal abuse, but for things like broken appointments too. Clearly you can't backtrack to day one, but you can make it clear that you are no longer prepared to be punished for things that are not of your making.*

35

Ashes to ashes

It's a dirty habit. Old dog ends, dropped ash, overflowing ashtrays, holes in your jumper. Disgusting, right? Cleaning up your act will cut down on the housework and say goodbye to yellow fingers and teeth.

None of us would choose to live in a burned-out building. The fire damage, charred timbers, ankle-deep ash, the smell of destruction. Yet as smokers we do just that.

Our world is dominated by burning leaves and poisonous smoke. It invades every pore of our being, from our smoke-soaked clothes and hair, to the stale stink of every piece of fabric in our houses from chairs to curtains.

SMOKE SIGNALS

Tobacco smoke carries one of those pervasive odours that you can mask but never fully hide. Pump as much of that ozone-eating spring-fresh flowery 'freshener' you like into the air and you'll still only achieve a layer of chemical gunk sitting on top of your poison cloud. It doesn't work. Cut down on the cigarette smoke and save yourself a fortune in airspray.

Here's an idea for you... **One by one, self-impose bans on other places you can't smoke. Advance slowly but surely so that you ban smoking progressively throughout the house, the car, your workplace etc. When you finally have your habit cornered, go for the jugular and stop.**

How many of us tried a sinful cigarette in our youth, fondly imagining that the tell-tale smoke would vanish with the first passing breeze? Anyone trying to fool their partner into thinking they've truly given up while sneaking the odd surreptitious quick one will know how futile this is. You're in this together – so talk to your partner, get their full support.

Not only do you pollute the air around you, the smoke clings to you like the proverbial unmentionable to a stick. Waft into a room and you bring with you the dull stink of your last smoke. Speak to someone without a three-yard buffer zone between you and they'll know before a word passes your lips.

Non-smokers have built-in detectors. Noses don't need to be subtle to smell smoke. It's a built-in self-preservation technique that goes back to the caveman. The species has long needed to know when the threat of going up in flames was imminent.

THE FIERY PIT

Imagine a warm summer's evening. You're relaxing with a glass of your favourite tipple when suddenly you smell smoke. How do you react to the stench of the neighbour's badly cooked barbecue drifting through your restful reverie?

Or that gloriously fresh morning when you've spring cleaned and every curtain, duvet and sheet is doing its impression of Admiral Nelson's fleet in full sail in your back garden. The first wisps of the helpful neighbour's garden bonfire cut across your bows like a fusillade of grapeshot. The washing might never have happened. The air is blue and so are you.

Explore ways to refresh your environment in IDEA 42, *Home, sweet home.*

Try another idea...

And does your gleeful heart ever stop to consider the heartache behind those fire-damage sales where you can pick up a bargain because the articles, while still perfectly usable, are deemed soiled goods because they've been subject to relentless clouds of smoke?

THE SWEET SMELL OF SUCCESS

If you've answered yes to any of the above, stop to consider the wilful smoke damage and threat of fire you knowingly volunteer for every day of your life by smoking in your house.

The answer is to practise damage limitation. If you can't do cold turkey you don't need to start a complete revolution – just advance slowly. Smoke is your enemy and it's invaded your house. Drive it out, pushing the frontline ever further forward.

Begin by banning yourself from smoking in certain rooms. The bedroom would be a good place to start. (You wouldn't believe the number of house fires that begin with a dropped dog end in the bed.)

Think public spaces and hygiene, and bar your cigarettes from the kitchen. Smoking and food

'Smoking is a custom so loathsome to the eye, hateful to the nose, harmful to the brain, dangerous to the lungs, and in the black, stinking fume thereof nearest resembling the horrible Stygian smoke of the pit that is bottomless.'
JAMES I of England, *A Counterblaste to Tobacco*

Defining idea...

Defining idea...

'Blow some my way.'
Chesterfield advertising slogan, 1926

have never been great bedfellows (kippers notwithstanding). Discover again the joys of cooking and its delicious aromas.

THE FINAL FRONTIER

The living room might be your final frontier. It's possibly the place where you most enjoy your cigarettes, relaxing in front of evening's television or watching a DVD. So now's the time to start watching more commercial television – adverts are tailor-made for a cigarette break. And for DVDs and videos there's the pause button.

Head for the great outdoors to savour your cigarette. And don't complain that it's raining or too cold. When has the weather ever deterred you from lighting up? Look outside any office building – smoking's not for wimps, we're a hardy lot. Be truthful, if we were astronauts we'd probably even take our helmets off for a smoke in the noxious fumes of the Alpha Centauri nebulae.

Once you're outside – no smoking inside any more – not only will you be giving your dwelling the chance to breathe in clean air and renew itself, you'll also be relieving your loved ones of the chance to die young with you by removing the risks of passive smoking.

Now you can begin to rediscover the joys of walking into a fresh smelling house. Each room will be smoke-free and unpolluted. The perfect time to become aware of (and tackle) those other annoying habits of leaving dirty clothes lying on the bedroom floor or failing to spot the half-eaten pizza under the sofa.

Reclaim your living space with new, improved air!

Q **My boyfriend smokes as well, so what's the point of me banning myself from smoking in different rooms is he doesn't?**

How did it go?

A *Good point. None at all. Time to work together and be real partners – and ban him, too. Apart from anything else, if you're intending to give up completely, you'll find it much easier if the whole thing is a joint venture and you both try to give up at the same time.*

Q **There is no outside to my flat unless I want to go down ten flights of stairs to get to the open air. What choice do I have?**

A *I'd give up as soon as possible. How are you going to manage all those stairs with smoker's lungs if the lifts break down? Seriously, you can at least limit your smoking to a certain room or only allow yourself to smoke in it between certain times. And don't avoid the stairs – a long trek down to enjoy a cigarette will make you think more about whether it's worth it.*

36

If you can't beat them, join them

The rest of the world is ganging up on smokers, refusing to share their space with us. Maybe it's time to throw in the towel and join the majority.

The anti-smoking lobby is on the march. They might be the enemy of contented smokers, but they could play a major role in helping you give up.

CHANGING TIMES

Remember when the majority of adults smoked and it was possible to smoke almost anywhere? You could light up in cinemas, in railway carriages, on buses, planes, underground platforms, in offices, factories, restaurants and pubs. In fact, go back far enough and smoking in these places was compulsory. But times, they are a-changing: now most adults don't smoke and this majority are increasingly ensuring that the environment is kept smoke free. Inch by inch, centimetre by centimetre, more and more public space has been converted into non-smoking areas. In committee rooms, debating chambers and wherever health & safety types ply their trade, plots are hatched to extend this blanket ban ever wider. The no smoking writing is on the wall everywhere: New Yorkers have been banned from smoking in

Take a leaf out of Cliff and Sue's book: make your home a no-smoking citadel. Post a No Smoking' plaque in a prominent place near the front entrance and, if questioned, tell visitors that you are keeping the smoking equivalent of an alcohol dry house.

bars and smoking is outlawed in public places as far apart as Italy, Cuba, Australia and even Iran. Ireland has prohibited smoking in pubs and bars; their smokers now have to smoke outside or in shelters erected especially for the purpose. And what has happened there is likely to spread, for example to the UK, despite all the obstacles the ingenious tobacco industry erects to prevent it.

INTRUSION ON FREEDOM?

For diehard smokers, restrictions and regulations feel like an intrusion on freedom. We don't need to tell you treating smokers as social pariahs is in itself counter-productive and will only add to the cool, edgy image the industry has been promoting for decades. But when you're giving up, a ban can be a blessing. Knowing you can't light up during a film or waiting for the tube can defer temptation. Being out of sight of other smokers lessens cravings. And the longer this goes on, the more you realise that perhaps you're not so badly hooked as you once thought.

Defining idea...

'There are some circles in America where it seems to be more socially acceptable to carry a hand-gun than a packet of cigarettes.'
KATHARINE WHITEHORN, British journalist

Many families have introduced a smoking ban within their homes, so that any members of the household and visitors who wish to indulge are obliged to go outside before lighting up. Recently one of us went to a party organised by our friends, Cliff and Sue. In the entrance porch of their impressive property was hung a huge 'No Smoking' sign. Something like this would have been unheard of a decade ago, but is likely to be an increasing feature of the brave new world we are moving towards. There are many reasons for this hardening of attitudes: effects of passive smoking on the health of children and everyone else, the desire to prevent cigarette burns on expensive furniture and floors, and the desire to keep the air as sweet as nature had intended are just three examples that spring to mind.

Try another idea...

Stuck in a party or other gathering where you are not allowed to smoke? Check out **IDEA 17**, *Suck it and see*, for suggestions about non-smoking nicotine alternatives like gum or patches.

THE TURNING TIDE

But even without legal bans and domestic by-laws, the tide is turning. Today's smokers can expect a frosty reception from increasingly unpassive non-smokers and even worse from ex-addicts, some of whom have replaced their nicotine fug with an air of smugness. The once cool image of cigarettes now seems tarnished, especially amongst professionals and in middle-class circles. It still has a grip on many, but there are fewer and fewer each year. Whether tobacco will become as unfashionable as opium and be replaced by something else only time will tell.

Defining idea...

'The immediate implication [of smoking bans] for our business is clear: if our consumers have fewer opportunities to enjoy our products, they will use them less frequently and the result will be an adverse impact on our bottom line.'
Philip Morris Incorporated

How did it go?

Q   My partner and I like the idea of having a smoke-free house but my two teenaged sons don't see why the ban should extend to their bedrooms. How can we convince them?

A   *Whose house is it? Yours. You pay the mortgage or rent and are responsible for making the rules. This is a brutal truth, but it was only hard, inflexible rules like these that gave our generation the get up and go to get up and leave home. You could go for a softer approach and tell them that you need their moral support in giving up the weed and that having smoke leaking out from under their bedroom doors undermines everything you are trying to achieve.*

Q   We put up a 'No Smoking' sign as you suggested and the indirect feedback we have got from some members of our extended family has been very unpleasant. Surprisingly, the person most put out is a non-smoker. Should we stick to our guns or take down the offending sign?

A   *That's families for you. They often hate change and will round on anyone who dares to rock the boat. Stick it out and weather the storm; next week they'll find something and someone else to bleat about.*

37

Sleeping with the enemy

Become a single-issue bore; make non-smoking your new addiction. Becoming a non-smoking guru could be your salvation.

You've almost managed to quit but are not quite able to go the extra mile? Raise your non-smoking profile and everyone will ensure you don't start again.

SERIOUS SINNERS MAKE THE BEST CONVERTS

You've tried the patches, gone cold turkey, chewed the gum (all five flavours), been to a hypnotist and you still can't stop. You've been for counselling – one to one and groups – had sessions of CBT (cognitive behavioural therapy) and you still can't stop. The shock of a parent's death from a smoking-related illness did stop you smoking, for all of 24 hours, but you still can't stop.

Maybe, just maybe, it's time to think the unthinkable, throw in your lot with the devil, swallow your pride and do the one thing you thought you'd never do: become a non-smoking bore.

In essence, non-smoking bores replace an addiction to nicotine with an addiction to pomposity: trading in smoking for smugness. It's a difficult one-way path with no

Here's an idea for you... **Bone up on all the famous people who've died of a smoking-related disease and use every opportunity to drop this knowledge into conversations.**

return, but others have gone there before and are only too happy to let everyone know they were chain smokers but have never had a cigarette or been tempted since that road to Damascus moment when their world changed.

BEFORE YOU START

You might be tempted to stop smoking straight away and immediately start spreading the non-smoking gospel. But wait. Is your current addiction bad enough? Pomposity is inversely related to the seriousness of your habit. Fifteen a day just isn't enough, Allen Carr, the role model for this sort of thing, claims to have been an eighty a day man. You'll have to dip into your pocket and spend serious money on cigarettes for a while, but it'll be worth in the long run; it certainly was for Mr Carr. Smoking this number will also improve your future street cred by making your seriously unfit, which should help you gain weight, in turn providing you with a great collection of slob 'before' pictures to use when trying to bore potential converts. Best of all, your increased consumption may give you a health scare and hopefully a short admission to hospital. Add in the stressful and damaging effect on your close relationships and you have all the ingredients needed to become a bore-again non-smoker.

Defining idea... *'The arguments about the effects of second hand smoke have been won and the [UK] Government accepts this. We urge the Government not to delay and ban smoking in all enclosed public places.'*
SAM EVERINGTON, GP and BMA council member

START SMALL AND BUILD

Converts to the church of non-smoking are advised to start modestly. Perhaps barely audible tut-tuts in the presence of a person with a lit kingsize. After a week or two, start wafting smoke in a histrionic fashion to induce maximum guilt in smokers and wonder out loud why smokers always hold their cigarettes away from themselves and closer to you. As your confidence increases you can start to glare at the person and mumble something about passive smoking. You'll need to bone up on this as it is the church's strongest weapon and needs to be cited at every available opportunity.

Tempted to become an anti-smoking ex-smoking bore but not sure if you could stomach the public gaze or tongue-twisting title? Have a look at IDEA 43, *Bonfire of your vanities*, for other, less controversial suggestions for bidding farewell to the cigarette.

Try another idea...

NOT MANY PEOPLE KNOW THAT

Dinner parties, social gatherings and conversations at work offer numerous opportunities to bring into conversation interesting facts and information about smoking and its effects. For instance, people are talking about their favourite films, someone mentions *Casablanca* and you chip in with, 'Did you know that Humphrey Bogart died of cancer of the oesophagus?' Royalty: the British Queen's father, grandfather and sister all died of a smoking-related disease. Someone is droning on about the wonders of psychoanalysis, you drop in that Sigmund Freud died of cancer of the jaw.

'People talk about 'giving up' [cigarettes] but you're not giving up anything.'
JACKIE KNOWLES, reformed smoker

Defining idea...

As you hit your stride these comments can be amplified and converted into mini-lectures. The cost of cigarettes is a good one: 'Did you know that if you hadn't smoked ten cigarettes a day for twenty years (at today's prices) you'd have saved enough to buy a small Japanese sports car? A packet of twenty a day for twenty years would get you something bigger and German, while giving up forty a day for fifty years would get you some serious real estate.'

ARRIVING WITH STYLE

You know you've arrived when you can confidently boast that giving up is easy. All that stuff about addiction is rubbish, a nasty rumour started by the industry. If giving up was easy for you then it ought to be easy for lesser souls. You will now be smug, self-righteous and insufferable. The people who once loved you will have long since stopped pleading with you to revert to smoking and become your former self. Telling everyone how easy it was to give up should make you deeply unpopular and might even induce your former friends and family to threaten you with violence. But even if they carry through their threats, you'll still have the secret pleasure of knowing that your dicky heart and knackered lungs are on the mend.

 How did it go?

Q   You guys are sick. I find this idea really offensive. Can't you come up with anything better?

A   *Maybe you're right, but we hope you agree that dying of a smoking-related illness is also pretty sick. And it's stupid.*

Q   Thank you. I was always reluctant to give up as I got so much pleasure smoking near non-smokers and party smokers and blowing toxic fumes in their faces. Thank you for providing me with such great ideas. I can't wait. I'm going to start right away. Can you see any problems?

A   *Not at all. You are just the sort of convert we need.*

170

38

This dog's got teeth

Tobacco smoke stains your teeth. Yes, yes, we know that. You can brush your teeth clean, but you can't brush your lungs clean. Yes, yes, we know that, too. Smoking makes your gums rot away and all your teeth fall out. Really?

Absolutely — see, you learn something new every day. I always saw a trip to the dentist as some sort of institutionalised form of torture. Until I met Yvonne, my dental hygienist.

SMOKING GUMS

Yvonne has changed the whole way I think about my mouth. She has also taught me a whole new way to clean my teeth. I thought, foolishly, that having done it for several decades I'd mastered the art of teeth cleaning, but oh no.

She pointed out that because I'd smoked for over 30 years I'd affected the bones of my jaw and as a consequence my gums were severely receded. This is known as peridontal disease and it meant that my teeth were losing the support they needed to stay in place – much like you watch a sandcastle being washed away and undermined by the incoming tide.

Here's an idea for you... **Consider a whole range of fruits, from grapes to strawberries, melons to cherries, sultanas to bananas. Go further and check out raw carrots, celery, sunflower seeds, etc. Choose a fruit and veg selection you enjoy and use these as nibbles whenever you feel the need to smoke.**

As a result, deep pockets have formed at the base of my teeth, and in these spaces bacteria have been free to have their evil way. This has further undermined the gums, which has opened up still deeper pockets, and – well, you can see the way things are rapidly heading.

Worse thing is my actual teeth are still pretty good. But, like a lonely drunk without a friend to hold them up, sooner or later they'll fall over. And I don't fancy adopting Gummy as a nickname.

A BRUSH WITH PERFECTION

'Giving up smoking is the single most important thing you can do to save your teeth and gums,' said Yvonne. This was echoed by Duncan the dentist, who had popped in to reinforce her message. You're five times more likely to lose your teeth if you smoke because the reduced oxygen in your bloodstream restricts the gums' ability to fight back.

Okay, so apart from that, what can I do while I'm working on giving up? First thing was to buy myself a really good toothbrush. This had to be electric because their speed means that they clean more thoroughly than a hand-powered one. And not just any old free-with-a-packet-of-cornflakes electric toothbrush.

Defining idea... **'Ask your dentist why Old Golds are better for the teeth.'**
Lorillard advert for Old Gold, 1935

You have to lay out a bit of cash – there are good deals at most of the big supermarket chains now – and buy the equivalent of Harry Potter's Firebolt broomstick. At the time of writing, I use a brush powered by a Braun 7000 motor. Just as soon as they work out a method of getting the toothpaste to stay on the damn brush as it whirls round like some astronaut's g-force machine it'll be perfect.

Gums are handy but we can just about live without them. Not so the lungs. Find out why in IDEA 21, *The air that we breathe.*

Try another idea…

SMILE THOUGH YOUR HEART IS ACHING

Which brings us to toothpaste. Sorry, leave those two-for-the-price-of-one deals on the shelf. It's got to be the real thing. Go for a recognised brand that's got an anti-bacterial ingredient to help combat plaque (a film of bacteria which causes peridontal gum disease).

And that's not all you can do. Floss. Flossing brushes come in a whole range of sizes to fit between your teeth (the closer the fit the better). They can get down deep between the teeth and clear away the bacteria from those deep pockets which your regular toothbrush just won't reach. You should use these twice a day.

Finally, invest in a good anti-bacterial mouthwash, not just to improve your breath but also to flush out any bacterial pockets. Peridontal diseases can never be cured but they can be slowed or stopped. So if you keep up the home treatment and visit your dentist regularly, you shouldn't lose any more bone beneath the gums.

'I would not put a thief in my mouth to steal my brains.'
CHARLES PORTIS, *True Grit*

Defining idea…

Follow all these ideas and, who knows, despite contracting lung cancer because you can't give up smoking, you might even make a good-looking corpse. And that'll be a great comfort to dear old Aunt Ethel, who'll be able to say proudly, 'But she still had all her own teeth, y'know.'

How did it go?

Q   I want to stop smoking and I'd like to try nicotine gum. The only problem is, it's like chewing old leather and my teeth aren't up to it any more. What can I do?

A   *There's a whole range of alternatives out there, Dan. If it's specifically nicotine replacement you're after, you could try patches instead.*

Q   With teeth like mine I know I'm never going to make it as a film star. When I smile it looks like a line-up of grime encrusted tombstones, so why bother?

A   *There are a number of smoker's toothpastes on offer which go some way to reducing the yellowing of teeth. Ask at your local pharmacy which might suit your needs best. Brushing regularly and flossing between the teeth is essential.*

Q   How can I tell if I've got gum disease?

A   *The simplest tell-tale sign is if your gums bleed when you brush or when you eat. Your breath might also become very unpleasant or you could find yourself developing abscesses. The best thing is to screw up your courage and get yourself down to the dentist for an X-ray.*

39

Do you smoke after sex?

Pay attention to this one. Which would you rather give up – sex or cigarettes? Sooner or later smoking is likely to win whether you like it or not. You'll be hard up without a hard on (yours or your partner's). Interested? Read on!

Sex is all in the blood. What flows through your arteries is what fuels your satisfaction. There's no question: smoking can seriously damage your sex life.

There are implications here for both men and women. With women, smoking has been shown to damage or destroy eggs, disrupt ovulation, screw up your menstrual cycle – particularly in middle age – and increase the risk of cancer of the cervix. Women who smoke are between two and three times less likely to get pregnant than those who don't.

Smoking when pregnant can cause damage to the unborn foetus, increase the probability of miscarriage, provoke premature birth and cause low birth weight. Smokers hit the menopause between 1 and 4 years earlier than their non-smoking sisters. They also suffer more hot flushes and are at an increased risk of heart disease and osteoporosis.

Here's an idea for you... **Take up meditation and learn how to instantly relax yourself. Use it every time you feel you want a cigarette. Because it focuses on breathing it concentrates the mind. Within a few minutes the craving to smoke will pass.**

STAND UP OR BE COUNTED OUT

A man's penis becomes erect when aroused because it fills with blood. It has no bones or muscles (though, interestingly, most other mammals, like rats and whales, do have a bone – the baculum. Now how fair is that?). Smoking causes the build up of fatty blockages in the small arteries that lead into the penis. The result? Less blood flows in and the erect penis is smaller and less hard.

If that's not bad enough, nicotine in cigarettes gives an instruction to the brain to make blood vessels contract more rapidly – this is called acute vasoconstriction, or vasospasm. This means again means that less blood can flow into the penis through the arteries and you could end up a flop.

It also means that blood cannot be retained as well by the penis – this is venous dilation, whereby the valve mechanisms in the veins don't function properly. If your penis can't hold in the blood you'd better be quick because your erection will be here and gone before you can do much with it.

...and another idea... **Treat yourself and your partner to a romantic night out with the money you've saved from not smoking. Push the boat out and go for a really expensive meal and a night in a romantic hotel. Don't worry about getting up for breakfast.**

Not only does smoking double your risk of impotence, but the fertility of your sperm can drop by over 50%, there's less 'come', reduced testosterone diminishes your sex drive, you won't be capable of having sex as often and you won't enjoy it so much when you do. So ask yourself, is it worth it?

SEX AND MORE SEX

Cutting down on cigarettes is clearly going to help but cutting them out altogether has got to be the ultimate answer. In the meantime we can use sexual pleasure as a tool to achieve this end.

Talk with your partner and, if they're willing, use sex as a cigarette replacement therapy or a reward system. There's probably going to be a limit to how amenable they'll be if you normally smoke sixty a day, but it doesn't have to be the full monty. Even a discreet fondle in a public place can be a very attractive alternative to a quick gasp, especially if it's merely a trailer for the three course feast on offer later if you don't smoke above, say, an agreed number.

Explore the other exciting things to do with your hands and other bodily parts in IDEA 49 Busy doing nothing.

Try another idea...

'Remember, if you smoke after sex you're doing it too fast.'
WOODY ALLEN

Defining idea...

STOP, THEN GO!

When you do stop you'll be amazed by the difference to your abilities. Within 72 hours your energy levels increase and your breathing improves. Less than three months later the blood circulation will have shown dramatic improvements.

And there's the money you'll have saved. Take your partner to visit a sex shop and buy both of you a treat you can try out when you get home. With more energy at your disposal, as well as longer and harder erections, there's all kinds of fun things you'll be able to do.

'In the UK, about 120,000 men in their 30s and 40s are needlessly impotent because of smoking.'
Comic Company, 'Sex and Smoking' leaflet

Defining idea...

177

You'll also be able to rediscover the sheer pleasure of kissing. Mouth to mouth with a smoker is like licking an ashtray. Your breath will smell sweeter and your sexy bodily pheromones (the so-called sex scents) won't be masked by tobacco stink.

Become a new, sexier you!

How did it go?

Q **That cigarette after sex has got to be one of the most pleasurable of all smokes. Why should I give that up?**

A *Like we said at the beginning, take your choice: sex or cigarettes. Ultimately smoking's going to win and you won't have the choice any more. Either you'll be impotent or you won't have the breath left to do it. Choose now and enjoy sex till you drop.*

Q **Sex as a replacement or reward therapy for not smoking is all very well but my partner's coming up with some very wild ideas. What do I do?**

A *Just goes to show how much more imaginative brain space is freed up when you're not fixated with smoking anymore. Only do what you're comfortable with, but sit down and talk with your partner so she understands what the problems are. Free up your own imagination and surprise her with a few alternative ideas of your own. It's amazing what you can do with a used toilet roll and some sticky-backed plastic.*

40
Older and wiser

There isn't a smoker alive who, if given the chance to turn back time, wouldn't refuse that very first cigarette. Older, wiser and iller, we know better now.

That pre-smoking person is still inside you. Imagine if you could sit them down and give them the benefit of hindsight — just what lessons would you be able to teach yourself?

YOUNGER YOU: You smoke, don't you?

OLDER YOU: Yes, but I wish I'd never started.

YOUNG: So why do you carry on?

OLD: I can't stop. It's a drug addiction.

YOUNG: Lots of people give up drugs, it can't be that hard.

OLD: You don't know what it's like, and I hope you never do.

YOUNG: Surely it's just a matter of willpower? If you want to give up enough, you'll find a way.

OLD: You're probably right.

YOUNG: So how did you get started in the first place?

Here's an idea for you...

Buddy up with a fellow smoker and quit together. Support each other with ideas and tips, always be on the end of a phone for one another. Ring up when you desperately want a smoke and talk each other out of it.

OLD: It seemed a grown-up thing to do. Smoking looked cool.

YOUNG: Did you enjoy it?

OLD: No, it was horrible. I felt sick and dizzy the first time I tried it. But lots of my friends smoked and I didn't want to be left out. So I stuck at it until I could smoke without coughing my lungs up.

YOUNG: You've always got a cough nowadays and you sound dreadful first thing in the morning.

OLD: It's an unnatural thing to do putting burning leaves in your mouth and sucking in the smoke. When you first start your body tries to tell you it's a stupid idea; by the time you've become an addict your body's screaming at you that you're killing it.

[Pause while Older You coughs violently]

OLD: I was suckered in by all the lies about how smoking was sexy and what a pleasure it was. And before I wised up I was well and truly hooked.

YOUNG: So you're saying don't even try it once?

Defining idea...

'You're gonna have a tough time getting people to stick burning leaves in their mouth, Walt.'
BOB NEWHART, 'The Introduction of Tobacco to Civilization' sketch

OLD: Got it in one. They're poison. They kill you. It's like committing suicide slowly and painfully. Everyone fools themselves that one can't hurt, that they're strong enough to quit any time they want. Except they never quite get round to it. And then they die.

We can all learn from history. Follow the sorry trail of tobacco's conquest of the world in IDEA 4, *Curse Sir Walter Raleigh*.

Try another idea...

YOUNG: How different do you think your life would have been if you hadn't started smoking in the first place?

OLD: I'd have lived longer. I know I'm going to die 5, 10 years earlier than I need to – if I'm lucky. I'll miss out on watching my children or grandchildren growing up. I'll leave my partner stranded alone, having given them the extra burden of caring for me when I get seriously ill. I'd have been healthier without any doubt. I'd have had a lot more money to do things with; by the time I die I could almost have bought a house with the money I've wasted on the weed.

YOUNG: So you've got nothing good to say about smoking?

OLD: No, it's a completely stupid thing to do.

YOUNG: I agree. Does this mean you're going to stop?

OLD: Bit late now, don't you think? The damage has been done.

YOUNG: But if you were me now, knowing what you know, you wouldn't start, right?

OLD: Absolutely. If I had my time again I'd never light that first cigarette, ever.

'I knew what they were doing to injure people, to get children addicted to this product so they have another customer for 10, 15, 20 years. Believe me, fighting this doesn't make you a hero. It makes you a human being.'
PATRICIA HENLEY, successful judgment against tobacco companies in Los Angeles courts, 2005

Defining idea...

YOUNG: If I can be strong enough not to start, you can be strong enough to stop. That first cigarette was hard to smoke, and I'm sure the last one will be even harder. But if you listen to what you've just said to me, you'll know it's the right thing to do. You owe it to us to stop now; it's never too late.

How did it go?

Q   **I don't want my teenage son or daughter to smoke, but there's a lot of pressure on them from their mates at school. I can't believe how many of their friends smoke. What can I do?**

A   *We were all young once. It's the duty of a teenager to rebel against the grown ups and try out the forbidden – it's their job. Try not to be too evangelical. The louder you say 'No!' the more likely they are to try it out: teenagers are like that. Find out from your children's school how much anti-smoking education they provide. If it's not enough, ask your doctor or local library. There's a lot of good leaflets available.*

Q   **I feel really guilty about smoking when my son desperately wants me to stop. It's almost like being a teenager again, having to sneak round the back of the bike sheds for a smoke. What's the answer?**

A   *Your son's got good sense and your guilt should tell you instinctively who's in the right. If not for yourself, you should seriously consider giving up for his sake. Having your dad around hale and hearty well into your adulthood is a great gift. It's all down to you whether you are going to be there for him as he grows into a man.*

41

Live long and prosper

If you die early or become disabled through smoking you're not the only victim. Don't want to be around for your children, watch them grow up, get married, have children? No? Then stop reading now.

Our children are probably the most precious things in our lives, and they're our gift to the future. As parents, we need to make sure that they have the guidance and support to help their passage into adulthood. As smokers, can we be sure that we'll be there?

When I asked my daughter (who's now 9) why she wanted me to give up smoking she told me: 'So that you don't get ill and instead of you smoking, you can spend time with me (and maybe Mummy).'

When she talked about when she's grown up she said: 'Even though I sometimes like lighting your lighter, it doesn't mean you shouldn't stop smoking. One of the things I want you to do when I grow up is stop smoking. You try very hard making me happy and you wouldn't be around to do that any more.'

Here's an idea for you... **Imagine you have been given the gift of adding a further 5 years or 10 years onto your life. Write down all the things you'd like to do with that extra time – and give yourself at least two thousand a year extra as spending money. (Stop smoking tomorrow and your dream may come true.)**

THINGS THAT COUNT

She has plans to get married and be a mum. 'I want you to help me bring up my children because I don't know how. I'd love my children to have a grandad. Most of all, I want you to be there as I get older. That's the thing that counts.'

And I won't be if I carry on smoking. My grandad died at 74 from lung cancer (after several years of bed-bound illness). My dad died at 83 from emphysema (after 10 years of wheezing around unable to walk more than a few yards without his nebuliser). My auntie died at 76 from emphysema (after 7 years of being attached to an oxygen tank, in between the cigarettes). My brother died at 55 from an aneurism/stroke (a heavy smoker all his life). So why should I last any longer? Why am I immune?

Defining idea... **'R.J. Reynolds has a long history of working to reduce the risks associated with smoking cigarettes. Smoking is addictive. The best way to reduce the risks of smoking, of course, is to quit.'**
R.J. Reynolds Industries website, 2005

WHEN I'M 64

If I get to 64, my daughter will be 20, at 74 she'll be 30, at 84 she'll be 40. I've often joked with her that my favourite number is 92. It would be great to survive that long; then she'll almost be as old as I am now (my grandad on my Mum's side died at 90, never smoked, and was still playing lacrosse in his 80s).

How about you? How important is it to you that you're around for your children as they grow up into adults? And do you want them to have to look after an invalid in your declining years? What about your partner, how will they feel struggling with someone unable to do anything for themselves and abandoned alone as they struggle through retirement?

Think of all the wonderful things you could do with all that extra cash. Read IDEA 46, Who wants to be a dead millionaire?

Try another idea...

GROWING UP

There are two issues here. You and your children. Your child will plead, 'Please don't smoke any more.' It's not only because they've been educated in school about the evils of smoking. It's also because they can see with their own eyes that you cough your lungs up every morning, that you can't play football any more (no great loss in my case) or run up hills with them like you used to. And they love you to join in.

It's also about you. You're an adult and you've lived long enough to be able to have a concept of the future. We really ought to know better because we know where our path is leading. Don't you want to be there for your child's wedding? Do you really want to watch your grandchildren play and grunt from your wheelchair as you reach for your portable nebuliser or draw your blanket up round the stumps of your legs?

We all need to grow up and realise our responsibilities as parents. They don't end when your child leaves home, they continue until the day you die. Why die early or in agony, and deny them and you all those years of additional pleasure? Carry on smoking and we're just being selfish.

'We do not want children to smoke.'
Imperial Tobacco website, 2005

Defining idea...

How did it go?

Q **My son comes home from school full of stuff about how smoking is bad for me, but doesn't understand how hard it is to give up. What can I say?**

A *Okay, it's your responsibility to tell him. It's hard to give up, no question – but it's not impossible. Millions have done it and so can you. Explain to your son how difficult it is to break any addiction. Sit down and decide what's most important, your son or your cigarettes. Get real: you choose.*

Q **It's easy for my partner. She gave up but she was only ever a casual smoker, so it was easy for her. She hounds me to death, and I just slink away and have another cigarette. How can I make her understand?**

A *Talk to her. Explain to her how your situation is different but then, most importantly, enlist her as a helper and show her how she can be your support in giving up. After all, it's in both your interests.*

42

Home, sweet home

Decorating your home is a great way to celebrate your decision to quit.

Spending cigarette money on home improvements will reinforce your desire to stop, making you popular with people who share your house or flat.

What, you might wonder, has decorating your home got to do with giving up the weed? In short, quite a lot. If you have been smoking inside, rather than in the garden, the legacy of your habit will be everywhere; the stink of stale tobacco will have permeated the curtains, carpets, walls and soft furniture. A fresh lick of paint or steam cleaning the three piece, carpets and curtains are ways of actively demonstrating your commitment to a new life, a life without cigarettes. And hopefully, having spent time, money and energy improving your property, you'll be less inclined to smoke inside again and return it to a state of nicotine-stained squalor.

During the transition period when you are quitting it is a good idea to stay away from the temptation of places like pubs and bars where other people are puffing. A newly decorated home will feel more welcoming and you are more likely to want to stay in.

Here's an idea for you...

Synchronise the date you stop smoking with a campaign to improve your home. You can use the money you would have spent on cigarettes to buy materials and tools. Working on your home will not only improve your physical environment but also burn up nervous energy when you are fighting cravings to smoke again.

HOME MAKEOVERS

We are not talking about a quick once over with a large tin of whitewash. What we have in mind is far more radical and enjoyable. A home makeover can be a thing you do for yourself rather than something that happens to strangers on daytime TV. Most large bookshops have a varied collection of 'how to' books, brimming with suggestions about how to transform a dump into a desirable dwelling. If you smoke twenty a day, a month's supply will buy you a small library of these books that will feed you with enough ways to improve your home making that you'll be the envy of your neighbours (and if that doesn't work, you can always use them as wallpaper). The cost of eighty cigarettes will buy you a decent step ladder, two hundred the cost of an industrial floor sander for the weekend or a cheap (but cheerful) power drill.

Before you get to the enjoyable creative bits, you have the less than edifying task of preparatory work. Painting over nicotine-soaked ceilings and walls is only a short-term solution, and sooner rather than later the brown sludge will penetrate through the new eggshell or emulsion. Fortunately, good old sugar soap has also had a makeover and now comes in a spray-on form, making it ideal to cut through the grease and provide the perfect key for new paint. Ceilings that have been tanned and remind you of an old pub will need sealing first. It's a

Defining idea...

'If you must smoke, take your butt outside.'
Anon.

188

messy process, leaving you covered in hard-to-remove waterproof glue, but worth it in the long run. And while you are seeing the damage smoke has done to your property it's worth considering what the same stuff, in a concentrated form, has been doing to your lungs.

While giving your home a spring clean, there will be lots of smoking-related junk to throw out. Check out IDEA 43, *Bonfire of your vanities*, and do so in style.

Try another idea...

THINK THE UNTHINKABLE

Houses and flats are only machines for living in. They are often things we don't give much thought to. A threadbare carpet is replaced by a new one; tired-looking wallpaper is replaced by fresh wallpaper, albeit in a newer, more modern design. It doesn't have to be so. A radical makeover means starting from scratch and reconfiguring your home so that it's fully adapted to your current needs. This might mean converting a spare bedroom into a home office or games room, enlarging the kitchen and using the dining room for snooker, or simply changing the focal point in the lounge. Painting a room in completely different colours can transform the way it looks and how you feel about it. Getting rid of clutter makes rooms seem more spacious, and regrouping your pictures or other objects could make them seem more impressive.

'Thank you for not smoking. Cigarette smoke is the residue of your pleasure. It contaminates the air, pollutes my hair and clothes, not to mention my lungs. This takes place with out my consent. I have a pleasure also. I like beer now and then. The residue of my pleasure is urine. Would you be annoyed if I stood on a chair and pissed on your head and your clothes with out your consent?'
Sign from Ken's Magic Shop

Defining idea...

189

Supplementing a lone ceiling light with a range of small, local light sources will also enhance the mood of any room and improve its function, be it a bedroom, kitchen or hallway.

Improving your home has a massive impact on your morale and self-confidence, and could be just the fillip you need when you are withdrawing from the dreaded weed.

How did it go?

Q   Why should we decorate our place? We rent it and it's the landlord's job, and we certainly pay him enough rent.

A   *Maybe you do, but wouldn't you like a say in how your home looks? You could ask him to provide the materials and still get stuck in. After all, you are the people who will benefit most. If you play your cards right, you could even live rent-free for a month in lieu of payment (not likely, I know, but we live in hope). And if you manage to quit smoking you might be able to put together enough money to get your foot on the property ladder.*

Q   I smoke outside. How is decorating my home going to make a difference?

A   *Even if you never smoke inside, decorating your home still divides two eras – a line in the sand, if you like, between the time you were a smoker and the time you came clean. Planning and painting will give you something to do physically and take your mind off your craving during the difficult withdrawal phase. You could also consider giving your garden where you used to smoke a makeover.*

43

Bonfire of your vanities

Every smoker's home contains an expensive collection of knick-knacks that support the habit. Serious about stopping? It's time to break up the collection.

Getting rid of ashtrays, lighters and other smoking accoutrements sends out a powerful message: you've passed the point of no return.

Look around your manor and you'll see evidence of your smoking habit. We're not talking about a nicotine-stained ceiling or cigarette burns on the sideboard, or even that cluster of butts outside the kitchen door; rather, ashtrays, be they glass ones, china ones or metal ones 'borrowed' from pubs, and lighters, iconic petrol designs, classics that double up as flame-throwers that singe your eyebrows, disposable ones you have never managed to dispose of, refillable jobs and their accompanying aerosol cans. Then there are cigarette cases (maybe you were given one when you turned 21), presentation tins that once held 200 Rothmans but now containing playing cards and chessmen, and tobacco tins that are now used to store screws and rawlplugs. We reckon it's possible to find smoking-related objects in almost every room in the house, whether it's a cheap and cheerful ashtray in the bathroom or tobacco tins in the tool chest under the stairs.

Here's an idea for you...

Round up everything in your house to do with smoking. Round up your family and friends, and get everyone to beat the hell out of these worthless objects. Kill the collection before cigarettes kill you.

Cigarettes, their makers and camp followers have managed to infest every part of your home. They are a constant reminder of the hold tobacco had, and maybe continues to have, on your life. Getting rid of this motley collection is about burning your bridges and passing the point of no return. It also sends out a clear message to your family, and especially your children, that cigarettes might have had a big part of your past but the little buggers are not going to have much of a say in your future.

When we say 'get rid of this collection' we're not talking about loading up the car and taking a trip to your local charity shop; rather, we envisage you physically battering the collection to bits, smashing china and glass ashtrays into three-dimensional 1000-piece jigsaws, converting tobacco tins and metal ashtrays into worthless but interestingly shaped scrap metal, and flattening lighters (empty ones, of course) with a sledgehammer. This might all seem a bit severe, especially if some of this stuff was given to you as presents. But the battle against smoking is bigger than that and if loved ones gets offended in the process, so be it. The Duke of Wellington arrived at a personal crossroads when in his late teens: whether to become a musician, like his father, or turn his back on music and become a soldier. He burnt his violin. Smashing your ashtrays could be your Waterloo.

START A TREND

Reducing this stuff to atomic particles is profoundly rewarding. A pleasure to be shared with friends and family. China-smashing stalls, once a firm favourite at school fetes, have been made a thing of the past in many places due to various institutionalised killjoys using a warped reading of health & safety regulations. Resurrect the custom in your back garden by getting everyone to throw heavy objects at your redundant ashtrays. Other families might want to contribute their own collections to keep the fun going. Taking turns to pulverise lighters or metal cigarette cases on the patio will, we promise, brighten your day.

JEWELS FROM JUNK

For the arty-farty types out there, you could always use the broken china to make a mosaic, or use tin snips to reconfigure tobacco tins into ear rings, necklaces and brooches.

BONFIRE OF YOUR VANITIES

Make a funeral pyre for your former smoking self. Start by making a 'guy'. This effigy should look and be dressed like you. If you can find an old jumper ruined with a cigarette burn, all the better. Ditto trousers and tie. Place a final kingsize in its mouth before placing it on a huge bonfire. For greater impact, wait until dusk before setting it alight. Send off your old habit in style.

Try another idea...

Having burnt your bridges you might be worried that you'll put on a few pounds. Read IDEA 7, *Fat is a former smoker's issue*, and weigh up the odds.

Defining idea...

'One thousand Americans stop smoking every day – by dying.'
Anon.

Defining idea...

'Much smoking kills live men and cures dead swine.'
GEORGE D. PRENTICE

How did
it go?

Q **What's wrong with giving cigarette cast-offs to charity shops? At least someone benefits that way.**

A *Do they? Eggcups, ashtrays and other tat hang around in shops like these until they close down. The only reason they don't throw them out is that these objects don't take up much shelf space. If ashtrays were the size of wardrobes, they'd soon be shot of them. And think: knowing what trouble you had beating your addiction, would you be happy knowing that your smoking paraphernalia was tempting others to carry on?*

Q **I've had to work hard for everything I own. Breaking things is so not me. Isn't there a better way?**

A *Why not give it a try? There is something very liberating about smashing things related to a habit like smoking. Just think of the damage that cigarettes have been doing to your body. This might not be getting back or getting even, but it's a start and it makes starting again that little bit more difficult.*

44

Trial separation

Time apart from your cigarette companions can help you make up your mind whether you want to stay in touch or not. Two weeks away could save your life.

Your relationship with those little tubes of tobacco isn't what it was. You want to get out but how can you leave? Space apart might be the answer.

GIVING UP IS HARD TO DO

You've got some leave booked, a holiday. You want to quit, well sort of, but aren't quite sure. You and cigarettes go back a long way. They've been part of your life for years, decades perhaps, always there ready in your pocket or handbag at times of stress, disappointment, celebration even. A gift you can give a homeless beggar to express your empathy, a casual way of striking up contact with a stranger or someone you wish to know better. Cigarettes are good for that and much more. But the cough is getting worse, friends think your older brother is in fact your son and non-smoking colleagues on the same pay band always seem to have more money than you. Should you take your cigarettes on holiday with you or put them in kennels?

Here's an idea for you...

No holidays due for a while? Not sure if you can commit to two smoke-free weeks? Then try a mini-break from smoking by taking your nearest and dearest to the seaside, a spa town or the hills for a couple of days. Instead of striking a match, strike up a conversation with a stranger. Every time you feel like lighting up, take a few deep breaths of clean air and feel deservedly smug. In just two days you'll significantly reduce your risk of having a heart attack and get the nicotine out of your system.

TAKE MY BREATH AWAY

Here are some reasons for using a holiday to toy with the notion of giving up smoking:

■ You're away from the glare of family, friends and ill-wishers.
■ You will be in the company of people who don't know anything about your smoking habit (or care).
■ You will be away from your usual routines and triggers that make lighting up almost a reflex action.
■ You will be removed from workplace stressors and tensions.
■ With luck, your holiday will be in a relaxed environment where other people will be paid to look after you.
■ You can arrange to be somewhere where hardly anyone smokes.
■ You have time to experiment with novel activities.
■ You can eat alternative foods away from the glare from people who know you.
■ Nobody who knows you need be aware of your experiment.
■ When you return from your break, any decision you arrive at will be informed by what you have done and learnt.
■ And if you do decide to give up, you will have got over the initial withdrawals before returning to your old routine and work.

Here are two different types of holiday to get you thinking

Big Apple or Emerald Isle

Ireland and New York are two places that have banned smoking in bars, pubs and most public spaces. Just what you need when you are trying to give up. Make either of these places the base for a social or cultural holiday. OK, in Ireland shelters and beer gardens are available for people who can't have a drink without a cigarette, but everyone else can enjoy a drink in a non-smoky place without the temptation of seeing someone else light up. If you choose the more distant destination, you'll have the additional advantage of a long (non-smoking) flight, which, added to the (non-smoking) wait beforehand, should set you well on your way to overcoming the first hurdle – the physical addiction to nicotine – thereby freeing you up to concentrate on the psychological aspects. You don't have to drink on your holiday, of course; indeed, there is such a strong link between drinking and alcohol that it is a good idea to moderate your drinking while attempting to give up. For the rest of the time you can be shopping, people watching, consuming the cultural treats, whatever takes your fancy.

Some people find that using blackmail on themselves has forced them to stop. If it works for them it might work for you. Why not look at IDEA 47, *Become a perverse philanthropist*, anyway?

Try another idea...

'Good food, good sex, good digestion, good sleep: to these basic animal pleasures man has added nothing but the good cigarette.'
MIGNON MCLAUGHLIN

Defining idea...

'The best way to stop smoking is to carry wet matches.'
Anon.

Defining idea...

Let's get physical

You don't have to go far to enjoy a holiday without cigarettes. There's a whole raft of activity-based holidays you can enjoy nearer to home. Pottery or potholing, judo or jewellery making, photography, wind surfing, scuba diving, the list is endless. Essentially, you get so involved in this pursuit that you'll be too knackered to even think about cigarettes during the day, and at the end of it you'll just be glad to hit the sack. Courses where physical effort is required will improve your fitness no end and get your lungs and heart working. Mostly these holidays are about learning new skills, improving existing ones and meeting new friends in a relaxed and informal environment.

How did it go?

Q   I'd love to go away on holiday on my own but I'm the main carer for my disabled mother. What should I do?

A   *Sounds like you both need a break. You could talk to your family doctor or local social services about arrangements for respite care. But talk to your mother first and see how she feels about it. Chances are she'll be only too please to think about you for a change.*

Q   I usually use holidays as a chance to stock up on cheap cigarettes. How can I resist the duty free?

A   *Just because you're having a holiday from smoking doesn't mean you have to skip all cheap treats. Why not spoil yourself and splurge on other duty-free treats, like chocolates and cosmetics?*

45

Duty free

Holiday madness. Half-price cigarettes, and who can turn down a bargain? You can. What's half of nothing? Nothing. That's what you'll spend if you don't fall down the duty free trap. Beware of bargains.

We spend maybe a couple of thousand for a fortnight of sun, and enjoy the cheaper drinks and cigarettes while we're away. The temptation is to carry on the holiday spirit (minus the sun) with a suitcase full of booze and smokes on the plane home.

When we sniff a bargain it's like putting on blinkers. If it looks like we're going to save money, we forget entirely how much more we'd save if we didn't buy it at all.

SPOIL YOURSELF

Holidays are supposed to be treats. They're rewards to ourselves for all the hard work we put in the rest of the year. And we deserve it. So why not use your money wisely instead of sending it up in smoke?

Here's an idea for you... **At the end of every week give yourself a reward for not smoking, or put aside the money for that extra-special holiday. Plan what you're going to buy and make it a special occasion. Have it gift wrapped.**

Explore the local shops and markets or the duty-free shop properly. They don't just sell cigarettes and alcohol. There's a whole range of other goods to choose from which are much cheaper without the taxes than at home. Buy perfume, chocolate, a high-quality digital camera, a personal stereo. Some of these items will continue being a source of pleasure to you for years to come. A cigarette lasts only a few minutes.

BE ADVENTUROUS

Part of the pleasure of going abroad is the opportunity to explore a different country and another way of life. You may simply want to cook yourself on the beach and go down to the local bar, but if your tastes are more adventurous all sorts of pleasures can be yours for the taking if you stop smoking.

Defining idea...

'If we see you smoking we will assume you are on fire and take appropriate action.'
DOUGLAS ADAMS

Do something you've never done before. Treat yourself to something exotic while you're away instead of wasting your money on cigarettes. It might be something produced locally, or particular to the culture, like clothing or pottery. It could be an extra trip out or two, scuba diving, deep sea fishing, or a top class meal at an expensive restaurant.

A TASTE OF PARADISE

If you saved up all the money you spend on cigarettes – both on holiday and at home – you could very easily have a substantial amount towards buying your own holiday home in the sun or a timeshare on some dreamy beach.

Why take all that smoke back home to pollute where you live? Look at IDEA 35, *Ashes to ashes*, to see what a mess we make.

Try another idea...

More immediately, the money you'd save in a single year from not smoking will go a long way towards paying for your holiday next year. Pick up a brochure at your local travel agent and start to plan now.

You'll have a lot more money to spend on that break than you ever had before, so why not pick somewhere completely new and exotic or luxurious? Or instead, you could take your normal holiday and use the extra money to take a second holiday later in the year. Alternatively, choose some favourite member of the family who can't afford to get away and take them along with you as a special treat for them (only non-smokers need apply).

AWAY FROM IT ALL

On holiday we can forget all the stresses and strains of everyday life and relax. For some it's the perfect opportunity to save money all the year round – by giving up smoking altogether.

It has the advantage that you're in unfamiliar surroundings without many of the triggers that would normally cause you to smoke. And without other things to worry about, you're free to concentrate on getting through those tricky first few days.

'Smoking is very bad for you and should only be done because it looks so good. People who don't smoke have a terrible time finding something polite to do with their lips.'
P.J. O'ROURKE, American humorist

Defining idea...

201

Stop smoking at the airport and vow never to set foot back home as a smoker again. Two weeks without cigarettes and you'll already have begun to feel the benefits of not smoking. Most of the serious cravings, caused by nicotine starvation, will have gone and your general health will have improved.

It will be a holiday to remember. You'll come back a new person. You'll also be able to show the strength of your commitment to the new you by walking straight past the cheap cigarettes and buying something else to make you feel good about yourself.

How did it go?

Q One of the pleasures of going abroad is being able to stock up on all those duty frees. It's like Christmas, isn't it?

A   *Becoming a non-smoker will be like ten Christmases rolled into one (plus you'll be alive to see them). There are plenty of other pleasures to do with going abroad. Spend the money you save on doing more of them.*

Q Why are cigarettes so expensive at home?

A   *Ask the government. Every packet of cigarettes is taxed by them, with the government taking the lion's share of what you pay for a packet. Other countries charge a lower tax so they're cheaper. The massive tax earned by you smoking brings in a huge revenue and is one of the major reasons why politicians are so loathe to bring in laws banning it. It would be cutting off the hand that feeds them, even if you have to have a lung cut out to pay for it.*

46

Who wants to be a dead millionaire?

Play the game of a lifetime (however short that may be). A thrill-packed adventure stuffed with prizes, from the holiday of a lifetime to a brand new car of your choice. But beware the booby prizes (only for boobies who smoke).

No game worth playing is all win—win. Except if you're a non-smoker, in which case you're the winner of this game before we start. All smokers are losers.

The objective of the game is to live as long as possible and keep as much of your own money as you can whilst going through life as a smoker. The more you cut down, the better your chances of success, and if you quit completely there are plenty of bonus points.

THE RULES

Go immediately to square one. You don't need a six to start. Anyone can start at any time without any help. The board represents a smoker's journey through life.

Here's an idea for you... **Draw a column of smoke with notches for every pack of cigarettes – like those fundraising thermometers outside schools or churches – and mark off against it what you could have bought instead of cigarettes.**

GAME FOR A COUGH

Proceed round the board. one square at a time. You'll have to slow down after about square 10 because your lungs won't let you go any faster.

Obey the instruction on each square. Throw a six on any square and you can quit smoking now.

If you give up smoking at any point in the game, go directly to the Lucky Jackpot box. Award yourself £2,500 (UK version) for every year you won't be smoking (saving on cigarettes, extra life insurance, cleaning bills etc.). Decide whatever luxury you want to buy with your savings. Congratulations, you're the winner!

If you're still smoking at square 20 go directly to the Death and Disease box. A prize every time! Throw 1 for Cancer, 2 for Heart Disease, 3 for Emphysema, 4 for Stroke, 5 for Impotence, 6 to Lose All Your Teeth. Hard luck, you're dead.

Try another idea... **Want to spend your money on something really worthwhile? Try IDEA 22, *Don't do that, do this*.**

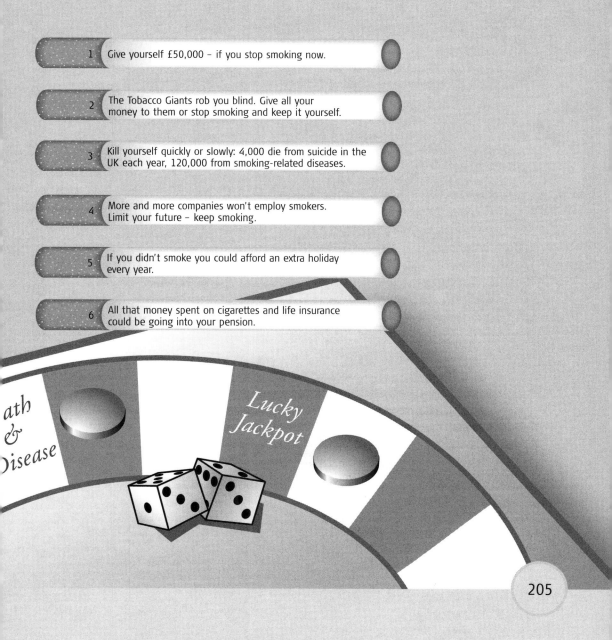

1. Give yourself £50,000 – if you stop smoking now.

2. The Tobacco Giants rob you blind. Give all your money to them or stop smoking and keep it yourself.

3. Kill yourself quickly or slowly: 4,000 die from suicide in the UK each year, 120,000 from smoking-related diseases.

4. More and more companies won't employ smokers. Limit your future – keep smoking.

5. If you didn't smoke you could afford an extra holiday every year.

6. All that money spent on cigarettes and life insurance could be going into your pension.

ath & Disease

Lucky Jackpot

7   You have less choice of hotels to stay in if you're a smoker.

8   Kill your family and friends through passive smoking while you smoke.

9   Give up sport. And walking. And breathing. Keep on smoking.

10   By now you'll have the early signs of a disease. Choose your favourite fast track to death.

11   Without cigarettes you could have bought yourself a luxury car by now.

12   Without cigarettes you could have bought yourself a caravan or holiday chalet.

13   Give up smoking now and enjoy 5–10 more years of life.

Lucky Jackpot

Death & Disease

'If you can't send money, send tobacco.'
GEORGE WASHINGTON

Defining idea...

14 | Cut down on smoking now and save up for your funeral. It'll be sooner than you think.

15 | Take out a second mortgage to pay for private health care to combat your life-threatening disease.

16 | Spend all your savings to buy all the stuff you need now you're house-bound through illness.

17 | Impotence and sterility threaten. Choose sex or death.

18 | Your children beg you to give up. Choose death or your children.

19 | Shame you smoked. By now your mortgage would be almost paid off.

20 | You don't have a choice any more. You're going to die horribly and soon.

'I'll give you a definite maybe.'
SAMUEL GOLDWYN, movie producer

Defining idea...

207

Q **I only buy low-tar cigarettes, I don't smoke very many and I make sure that I never smoke in the house. I think I'm managing very well – for me smoking's more a hobby than a habit. I'd not save much if I stopped and I'd lose one of life's little pleasures, wouldn't I?**

A *You could save your life if you stopped smoking, of course. And is it really such a pleasure? Really? You could be spending your money on much more enjoyable things or putting it into a pension so that your (longer, healthier, non-smoker's) retirement could be that bit more comfortable.*

Q **When I do my sums and work out how much I'd save by giving up cigarettes, it hardly seems worth it. It would take me years to save up enough to make it worthwhile. Why bother?**

A *You're only 20; think about this. If I were to offer you a cheque for around £60,000 when you got to 65, what would you say? Even if you only smoke one packet a day, that's roughly how much you'd save at today's prices.*

47

Become a perverse philanthropist

You've tried sensible ways of giving up and you're still puffing like there's no tomorrow. It's time to utilise your negative demons.

All of us know organisations or individuals we'd love to see do badly. Pledging money to them might just spur you into stopping.

Most of us like to think that we feel warmth and kindness towards our fellow humans and wish them no harm. We have a relaxed attitude to organisations like single-issue pressure groups, extreme political parties, cults, religions, advertisers, geeks who generate internet spam, talentless types famous for being famous; in short, anyone trying to influence us or take our cash. They are, we muse, all part of the rich tapestry of modern life and we would be the poorer without them.

We also know that this is utter bollocks. There are people in the public eye whose downfall would induce extreme pleasure, arrogant football clubs we'd love to see relegated and companies we pray might, just might, go bust.

Here's an idea for you...

If you're money rich and time poor, having to spend your insufficient off-duty periods doing humiliating work should you fall off the non-smoking wagon could be a great way of keeping yourself motivated. The prospect of having to spend Sunday mornings clearing litter from your local park while others languish in bed or go down the pub might just help keep you in line.

THE POWER OF HATE

This idea looks at ways of harnessing these negative bits of your inner world, using the motivation of hate to help you quit smoking. It doesn't matter whether a dislike for, say, (Lord) Jeffrey Archer is driven by envy of his literary skills, wealth or choice of wife, or a natural antipathy towards his political views or self-promoting stunts. What matters is that you have identified a focus and someone who it would hurt you to give serious money to.

Again, you may feel irritation or even anger with a small charity that preys on the vulnerable, exploiting a sentimental love of animals to get the elderly to leave a little something in their will for a donkey sanctuary. If you were robbed of your rightful inheritance by just such a ploy when Great Aunt Maud died, recall the murderous feelings you felt at the time and imagine how much worse you would feel if you compounded the hurt and rubbed salt in the wound by giving the sods even more money, and money you can't afford? Now how's that for motivation?

HERE'S HOW

Find your target

You might be lucky and just reading the passage above could generate a name. If not list people or organisations that irritate you and try to identify what it is about them that gets under your skin. This might lead to a more promising subject. Conversely, you could scribble down the names of teams you love and consider pledging money to their greatest rival. For example, if you support a political party on the left you could identify a rampant neo-Nazi outfit who'd just love to have a donation from you. If you are still struggling, you could always ask a friend; they'll be sure to remember at least some organisations you've ranted on about.

Want to consider other ways of motivating yourself through money? Take a look at IDEA 14, *Money makes the world go round.*

Try another idea...

Locate contact details

Making contact with someone in the public eye is remarkable easy. Most high flyers have an entry in tomes like *Who's Who*, available at your nearest reference library. Alternatively, pumping their name into a search engine should reveal something on the internet. If they have written a book, their publishers should be happy to pass on snail mail. Again, searching the internet for a company, political party or organisation should readily unearth contact information.

'A cigarette is a pipe with a fire at one end and a fool at the other.'
Anon.

Defining idea...

Make a contract

Your contract of payment needs to be specific, witnessed and signed. 'I, John Brown, promise that if I have started smoking by 24 July 2006 I will send the enclosed predated cheque for £1000 to the British National Party and ask to be added to their mailing list. Signed in the presence of my fellow left wing friend Joan Green.'

'The public health authorities never mention the main reason many Americans have for smoking heavily, which is that smoking is a fairly sure, fairly honourable form of suicide.'
KURT VONNEGUT

Defining idea...

Write and date a cheque and put it in the custody of someone who promises to grass on you if you revert to smoking.

Carry a copy of this contract around with you, wrapped around a packet of twenty. Read it every time you feel the urge. Visualise the pleasure and help your unsolicited gift would give to someone or something you intensely dislike.

How did it go?

Q   Thank you very much. I used one of your examples and sent £100 to a donkey sanctuary when I relapsed. Now I am being bombarded for more donations. Where did I go wrong?

A   *Sorry about that. It seems to us that by using one of our suggestions rather than thinking up your own your motivation wasn't as strong as it could have been. But it sounds like you're starting to build up an unhealthy head of steam over the begging letters, so perhaps it's working after all. Why not pledge £1000 next time?*

Q   I'm intrigued, but I don't think I feel consistently strongly about my irrational hatred of men who comb hair over a bald pate to keep myself motivated. Am I barking up the wrong tree or just barking?

A   *A bit barking, but perhaps not barking enough. Disliking comb-over haircuts has possibilities, but were you to hate men who wear wigs you could have a much better focus. However, a stronger incentive need not cost you a penny but could be a lot more painful: shave all the hair from the crown of your head and cultivate your very own hateful haircut if you don't give up.*

48

Don't give up giving up

Quitting for good might seem like climbing Everest. With careful planning, Everest is climbed all the time, and sometimes without oxygen masks.

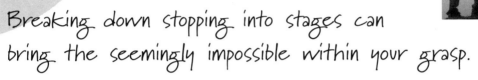

Breaking down stopping into stages can bring the seemingly impossible within your grasp.

Why did you start smoking? To fit in? To look cool? To be grown up? What still applies? What else have you found that smoking does to you, and is it nice? Only you will know the answers to these questions, so why not jot them down? Once you have a list of all the reasons why you want to give up smoking, put the list in your packet and read it through before you light up. Don't deny yourself any cigarettes at this stage.

PREPARING TO STOP

Mess around with your usual smoking routines. If you usually smoke last thing at night, take the dog out for a final walk instead. If you have two smoking breaks at work, try having them both in the morning and introduce a tea break in the afternoon. At this stage, you don't need to focus on smoking any less, just mess around with your habit. Once you've changed your habits, it's easier to break them.

Next you'll be ready to pick a quit date on your calendar and circle it in your favourite colour. Select your preferred way of quitting (there should be at least one

Here's an idea for you...

When you relapse, it's tempting to think of it as an all-or-nothing failure. 'What the heck, I've had one, I may as well smoke the whole packet.' Nothing could be further from the truth. If you smoke one cigarette, that's all you've done, smoked a measly cigarette. Why let it beat you? The fewer cigarettes you smoke and the sooner you think about stopping again the better. After all, practice makes perfect.

Brilliant Idea that appeals to you) and buy any aids you might need, like nicotine gum or dried fruit. Set yourself some goals. It's important that they're specific and attainable. For instance, the goal 'I want to be a non-smoker for good' may be too non-specific and difficult if you've been a heavy smoker all your adult life. 'I want to get through the weekend without smoking' is a more realistic start and means you won't be setting yourself up to fail.

Recruit friends and family, and tell them of your intentions. Be really clear about what you expect from them by way of support. Are you looking for loved ones to be firm with you if your resolve wavers, or will that just draw you into unproductive arguments? Many people find it helps if their families take a positive caring stance without being too judgemental if things don't work out at your first attempt or even fortieth.

Defining idea...

'It's a little like wrestling a gorilla. You don't quit when you're tired, you quit when the gorilla is tired.'
ROBERT STRAUSS

Compile a list of useful numbers and keep them by the phone for crisis times ahead. Numbers you might like to have handy are your local quitline, any friends who are also giving up and successful ex-smokers who'll know exactly how you feel and how to get through it.

STOPPING

Try to make your quit date as relaxed and stress free as possible. You might like to have a day off and be pampered at a health farm, or you may prefer to throw yourself into work and distract yourself from smoking as much as possible. Whatever you decide, it's vital that you throw away all your cigarettes. No ifs and butts. You've passed the point of no return. It's also time to bin all your lighters and matches. You might want to give the pub a miss for a few weeks, as drink often dilutes the most steadfast resolve.

Having trouble staying stopped? Why not overcome temptation by going to IDEA 50, *Stay stopped*?

Try another idea...

STAYING STOPPED

You've done the hard bit, but now you've got to stay strong and stay motivated. Remember why you gave up in the first place; feel proud in what you've achieved so far; change your routine to avoid those smoking triggers; and put the support network that you set up to work.

'It's always too soon to quit.'
NORMAN VINCENT PEAL, positive thinking guru

Defining idea...

RELAPSING

Relax. These things happen. Many ex-smokers gave up several times before managing to stay stopped for good. The most important thing you can do is recognise it for what it is – a temporary lapse – and start thinking about stopping again. Use your past attempts to help future efforts. What worked

'Remember you did not enjoy being a smoker. That's why you stopped. You enjoy being an ex-smoker.'
ALLEN CARR, non-smoking guru

Defining idea...

215

last time? How did you successfully cope with cravings? What are the social pressures that make you reach for a smoke? When you gave up last time, how did you cope with your smoking triggers without smoking?

How did it go?

Q **I've been here before and it always ends in tears after a few weeks. How can I convince my friends, and especially my long-suffering partner, that this time I'm stopping for good?**

A *You can't. All you can do is demonstrate that this time you have a good plan and that you are serious about trying to stick to it. Being open about past failures and using the people who know you best to help you understand the times when you are most at risk certainly should increase your chances.*

Q **I want to give up but I am not sure whether I'm ready to. Should I try or do you think I should put it off until I am more convinced?**

A *You expect us to say give it a go, and you'd be right. Giving up is never going to be easy; indeed, it is likely to get harder the longer you leave it. Get out now, while you can. There really is life after smoking.*

49

Busy doing nothing

There's time on your hands. There's an addict inside you begging you to have just one last cigarette. Stay active. Scan this handy survey of replacement activities and choose your weapons.

Smoking actually takes up an impressively large chunk of your life. Buying cigarettes, finding your lighter, smoking the damn things, coughing. What could you do instead with all that time?

It's important to see this extra time as a gift rather than a burden. The extra years of life you'll gain are easier to deal with because you can plan larger projects. With the extra money you'll save there are opportunities for holidays, redecorating the house or flat, redesigning the garden, choosing interesting courses to go on.

The more challenging aspect of extra time is on a day-to-day basis: all those five minutes not spent smoking.

Here's an idea for you... **Celebrate the new you with a calendar of fresh ideas. Draw up a list of 52 new things to do in the coming year, one for each week.**

SMOKELESS FUEL

If you take cigarette breaks at work, the chances are you'll be hanging out with the smokers behind the bike sheds (or wherever you and your evil habit have been banished by the company). Not having to do that any more can afford you the time to meet new people and mingle with the non-smokers.

Then there's all those novels you can read, slotting chapters into the odd five minutes here and then. Or you could sit somewhere quiet and savour a few tracks on your personal stereo or iPod. You could even take up the art of letter (or postcard) writing (remember that?) again and pen some lines to long-lost friends.

Crosswords or puzzles could easily fill the void. Or set yourself the task of learning new words – in a language of your choice – and carry a little pocket dictionary around with you. Instead of walking to the shop to buy cigarettes, walk to the shop (after all, it is good for you) and buy a magazine you wouldn't normally buy.

There are many other ways to enjoy your new-found time: take up a hobby, learn a new skill, discover the artist or poet inside you, find a sport you'd like to play (you'll soon have the lungs for it), do all those jobs around the house that you've never got round to.

Defining idea... **'Reach for a Lucky instead of a sweet.'**
Advertising slogan for Lucky Strike, 1936

FOOD FOR THOUGHT

Food is a great replacement for cigarettes. Though not just any old food, unless you want to look like the Michelin Man. With your taste buds returning to normal you'll be able to relish the pleasure of fine food, but you will need to keep a weather eye on the calorie content. Smokeless and fat free is the new you.

Fresh fruit and vegetables (you need five portions a day anyway) are great for experimenting with. Prepare them and carry them in a snack box to dip into whenever you fancy. Fruit or herb teas (without sugar) can also help your palate to explore your new sense of taste.

OLD HABITS DIE HARD

Make the extra time work for you. Expanding your interests and taking on new challenges will help to break up the patterns of the old, smoking you. The habit of smoking clings to familiar rituals like smoke to clothes. Change your routines, do things differently, be novel and adventurous.

Go to work by another route or method. Alter your daily sequence of activities. Reinvent your weekends. Uncover the new you who doesn't smoke and become a hundred times more interesting as a person.

Have a good think about how much (or how little) life you've actually got left if you continue smoking. Read IDEA 29, *The sweet smell of success*. Aren't you cleverer than that?

Try another idea...

'I kissed my first girl and smoked my first cigarette on the same day. I haven't had time for tobacco since.'
ARTURO TOSCANINI

Defining idea...

How did it go?

Q   **I can't believe how fidgety my hands have become since I stopped smoking. It's like I've gained an extra pair of limbs I didn't know I had, and I've got no idea what to do with them. What's the answer?**

A   *Smoking is very bound up with the hands and mouth – they're the smoker's home-grown tools that make smoking possible. Take away the cigarettes and they have a lot less to do. Idle hands constantly remind us of smoking. You can retrain them over time, but in the short term try carrying round a pen and paper to doodle with. Alternatively, you could buy worry beads or one of those executive toys to keep them busy. Buy a drum, like a djemba, and learn to play. Take up model-making or painting. Book yourself in for a hand massage. Give your hands treats.*

Q   **My life was always organised around cigarettes – I'd smoke before or after activities, and sometimes while I was doing a task to aid concentration or as a reward. It was like I could set my watch by my cigarettes. Without them I feel like I've lost the signposts in my daily routine. How will I cope?**

A   *This lost feeling will pass in time. You need to focus more on the activities themselves. They have their own natural signposts – the act of smoking a cigarette was merely attached to them. If it would make it easier in the short term, try carrying around a packet of mints and have one of those instead.*

50

Stay stopped

Nicotine is always waiting round the next corner to ambush you, so you need to keep reminding yourself about why and how you gave up. Train yourself to become a non-smoker.

Giving up will doubtless be for a mix of reasons, from health to wealth and family. Knowing why you want to give up helps reinforce your resolve. Reminding yourself why helps you stick to it.

As you prepare to stop smoking, let's recollect some of the key elements you need to have in place. But never forget: first, YOU HAVE TO WANT TO. If you don't, then nothing will work.

REASONS TO BE CHEERFUL: ONE, TWO, THREE

A friend of mine, Susan, is an educated woman who works for a charity. She has a child who will need her continual support well into adulthood and most probably beyond. She wants to be around for him, but is finding it impossible to drop the cigarettes. 'I've read all the books and nothing works,' she says.

221

Analyse your habit. Write a list of when you smoke and why. Remember you're a smoker who really wants to stop.

She asked me to send her a copy of this book when it was finished. Hopefully the range of options that we've laid out will mean that she, like us, will find the right mix of approaches to kill her smoking demon before it kills her.

MORE THAN A MATCH

Life is made up of patterns, and humans love to tread those comforting, familiar paths. Smoking is one such ritual, each cigarette a little cycle of actions we grow accustomed to. Step out of the comfort zone for a moment and investigate.

What you must do more than anything is disrupt those patterns that trigger the desire to smoke. Get rid of all the smoking paraphernalia that litters your life. Change the ways you do things, especially anything that you can connect to smoking – where you sit, how you use the telephone, what order you do things in.

Break up the smoking pattern, create a new non-smoking one in its place.

YOU'VE GOT A FRIEND IN ME

Support is a vital ingredient in the recipe for success. A 'quit smoking' group, friends, colleagues at work, but particularly members of your family, can provide the extra discipline and morale boosts to keep you on the straight and narrow.

Having others to encourage you will make a big difference to your chances of success. They'll want you to quit and be proud of you when you do.

WALK THE WALK

You've talked the talk, now walk the walk. Prove to everyone you're bigger than the habit. Celebrate each new day, the increased money, the improved health. Live to 100 and patronise the other 'mere' pensioners.

There's a terrible sense of defeat about continuing smoking even though you know you want to stop. Your sense of self-esteem in rock bottom. The good thing is that the opposite is true when you do stop. You'll feel great and glow with the sense of achievement.

ONE DAY AT A TIME

You're a smoker, even when you've stopped. Just a smoker who happens not to smoke any more. So every day you'll have to face not having that first cigarette.

It's a bit like being an alcoholic. Those deeply ingrained paths still exist inside you and the Tobacco Demon never completely goes away. He's always lurking in the shadows waiting to waylay you like the Big Bad Wolf, and lure you back into his evil ways. Be strong every day. Resist. Remember one cigarette is never going to be enough; it'll be the first of many, the first of thousands.

Write down all the reasons why you want to give up smoking. Remind yourself why it's such a good idea.

Try another idea...

'The extraordinary rise in tobacco use [is] the single most important cause of the rising incidence of lung cancer.'
FRANZ HERMANN MULLER, 'Tobacco Misuse and Lung Carcinoma' (the first major report linking smoking and lung cancer)

Defining idea...

'I'll go to a club [in Britain], but you guys smoke so friggin' much, I can't sing for ages after. If everyone in England stops smoking cigarettes then I'll come and party.'
MARIAH CAREY, singer

Defining idea...

223

Believe in yourself. You are stronger than your addiction. You're not going to be fooled any more, be a slave to the profiteering giants of the tobacco companies, or fill the government's pockets with any more wasted money.

Promise yourself you'll never, ever start again.

How did it go?

Q   I really tried hard and stopped. It was like a miracle. Then one month later I had a stressful situation and I reached for the crutch and started again. I'll never be free of it, will I?

A   Nonsense! Courage, mon brave. Congratulations are in order. You gave up once and you can do it again. Remember Robert the Bruce and the spider.

Q   All my friends still smoke and I feel the odd one out. They even tease me about it, and make me feel as if I'm not grown up. What can I say?

A   Believe me, you're more grown up than them if you've stopped smoking, Chrissie. What's more, you'll grow a lot older and last a lot longer than them. Be proud that you've made the best decision of your life and stand up for what you believe in. Don't follow the crowd, think for yourself.

51

One can't hurt?

One cigarette isn't just one – it's the first of many. As soon as you light up you've stepped on the old treadmill, through those revolving doors and back into bondage. One is too many: you're an addict.

If, like me, you've attempted to give up, you'll know the feeling all too well. I've cracked it, I'm an ex-smoker, and to prove it I'll just smoke one. See? And if you don't believe me, I'll do it again.

Don't delay stopping. You're fooling yourself (and nobody else) if you put it off. And once you've stopped, stay stopped. Any other choice and you're simply giving in to your addiction. Be an ex-smoker the instant you've smoked that last cigarette.

CHAIN REACTION

One thing leads to another. For smokers never a truer word was spoken. Why settle for one when you can have two? The first one or two you'll cadge off friends, smokers who are more than happy to have you rejoin the fold.

Here's an idea for you...

Starting today, don't throw away a single butt. Become an instant collector and save up all your dog ends (carry a handy bag to pop them into). Find some see-through plastic containers and begin your collection. Empty all your ashtrays into them. Display them prominently.

Then you'll find yourself wanting some of your own. But you'll be good, you'll only buy a packet of ten. You'll set limits, fooling yourself that this time you'll control the habit, not the other way round. You won't smoke before midday, you'll ban smoking from the car or the house, you'll consciously choose not to smoke after a meal or with a drink. You'll manage on two a day.

And two will become five, and five will become ten. You'll have lots of good reasons why it's okay. Besides, tomorrow you'll go back to two. And, of course, you can quit any time you want. But you never do. Then the day will come (and it won't take long) when you buy that first packet of twenty.

MAÑANA

Never do today what you can put off until tomorrow. By the time you're back on to buying packs of twenty, believe me, you're a smoker again. You won't be able to just stop, you'll have to go through the whole process of stopping again.

And you won't be in the best shape to do it. You'll feel defeated, disappointed in yourself, a failure. If you're not careful you can convince yourself that this proves it: you'll never be able to give up, so why fight it?

That's the Smoking Demon in you talking. And if you do wake up one day and feel angry with yourself for caving in and decide to give it another go, the Demon will agree with you. At the same time he'll point out that you've still got most of a pack left, so why not smoke those while you're setting up your next attempt? Tomorrow will do just as well as today.

And then you'll buy another packet without thinking. Or agree with the Demon that this time you'll really do it properly. And that needs planning. So why not set a date next month, or on your birthday, indeed any date which isn't today? And to celebrate your new resolve, go out and buy a multipack of 200 and promise yourself you'll stop at the end of those?

Within a couple of months or less you'll be back smoking as many as you ever did – if not more. All your little controls and bans will have been swept away in the tide of addiction. It'll be like you've never stopped. And all because of one cigarette.

PARASITE LOST

Stop fooling yourself. Any delaying tactic is simply a big lie you're telling yourself. One cigarette is too many. The parasite living inside you is selfish and, like many parasites, it'll eventually kill its host (you). Kick out the parasite, kill your Smoking Demon and reclaim your life.

But do it now, do it today. And don't reach for just one more cigarette while you decide.

The smoker's mind works in devious ways. Don't listen to it; look at IDEA 20, _Smoke screen_.

Try another idea...

'Smoking is associated with longevity...this impairment is proportional to the habitual amount of tobacco usage by smoking, being great for heavy smokers and less for moderate smokers.'
RAYMOND PEARL, pioneer in the study of longevity

Defining idea...

'[They] are, in effect, mass killers. They are committing genocide by their products.'
JOHN CRONIN, British MP and consultant surgeon

Defining idea...

How did it go?

Q **I gave up for ten years. Then one day, after a big shock, somebody offered me a cigarette and I lit up without thinking. Now I'm back smoking again. I feel so depressed, I didn't realise I was so weak. How can I face myself?**

A   *Hang in there. If you did it once, and for so long, you can certainly do it again. If at first you don't succeed, try, try, try again. Don't blame yourself, it's one of the hardest things you'll ever have to do. Be determined. Consider the last attempt as a practice. Study what worked for you last time and what didn't. Then try again. You can do it.*

Q **I can't believe how hard I have to try to stay stopped. It's like there's two of me and the stronger half is always trying to tempt me to smoke, and I get so irritable. It's driving me and my partner mad. Should I trying smoking just once in a while when it gets really bad?**

A   *No! It's a trap and the start of the slippery slope. Each smoker has his own Dr Jekyll and Mr Hyde. Mr Hyde will tell you he'll be hell to live with without his cigarette. Just one will keep him happy (oh no it won't!). Call his bluff, talk to your partner, accept you'll be a pain in the arse and find other ways to deal with it. It'll get easier as Mr Hyde gets weaker. Persevere.*

52

Dog ends

Each day you don't smoke takes you further on the road towards reclaiming your life and your health. Check out the fantastic benefits week by week, month by month as we flag up the landmarks you will pass.

Kicking the weed will be the best thing you've done in years. You'll feel better in so many ways. As time goes by you'll wonder how you could ever have been so stupid as to start.

Celebrate. You've stopped; you're an ex-smoker. Get a calendar and mark off the milestones of success as they appear. Your future is going to be longer and better than you could ever have imagined. Let me count the ways.

Quite apart from the fact that you're richer, you don't smell as bad, you're more employable (lots of companies don't like smokers), your food tastes better and your sense of smell has improved, your self-esteem is on a high, the chances of your loved ones not suffering from passive smoking drop dramatically and, last but not least, there's your health.

Here's an idea for you...

Choose a wall in your house or flat. Paint it white. Buy a permanent marker pen. Keep an exact count of how many cigarettes a day you smoke. For each one smoked draw a dot on the wall. See how long it takes to turn the wall completely black. Then it will match your lungs.

GIVING UP: THE HEALTHY OPTION

- 20 minutes after smoking your last cigarette your heart rate drops.
- 12 hours after quitting the carbon monoxide level in your blood drops to normal.
- 2 weeks to 3 months after quitting the risk of you suffering a heart attack begins to drop. Your lung function begins to improve.
- 1 to 9 months after quitting your coughing and shortness of breath decrease.
- 1 year after quitting your added risk of coronary heart disease is half that of a smoker's.
- 5 years after quitting your stroke risk is reduced to that of a non-smoker's.
- 10 years after quitting your chance of developing lung cancer is about half that of a smoker's. Your risk of cancers of the mouth, throat, oesophagus, bladder, kidney, pancreas and cervix decreases.
- 15 years after quitting your risk of coronary disease is back to that of a non-smoker.

LOW RISK

As an ex-smoker you have considerably reduced your risk of:

- Strokes
- Cancers of the mouth, throat and oesophagus
- Cancer of the larynx (voice loss)
- Chronic obstructive pulmonary disease
- Ulcers
- Bladder cancer
- Peripheral artery disease
- Cervical cancer
- Low-birth-weight babies

ADDED BENEFITS

- You won't make fat cat tobacco company executives any richer.
- You won't be handing over any more of your hard-earned pay than you have to in taxes to the government.
- You'll be sexier (in more ways than one).
- You'll be able to play the piano (I lied about that one, but you might now have enough time left to learn).

Okay, flaunt the fact that you're a non-smoker. Read IDEA 37, *Sleeping with the enemy*, and learn how to harass the enemy: the smokers of this world.

Try another idea...

'They're know they're selling death now. They're not stupid. They just don't choose to admit it.'
SIR GEORGE GODBER, UK Chief Medical Officer for Health, 1960–72

Defining idea...

Defining idea...

'Comes meus fuit illo miserrimo tempo (It was my comfort in those miserable times).'
SIR WALTER RALEIGH (inscription on his tobacco box, found in his cell after his beheading for treason, 1648)

RELAX, DON'T DO IT

Any recovering drug addict feels stressed. What you don't need to do is head back into the same old habits to relieve the stress. Addicts who've gone through treatment in prison are strongly encouraged not to go back to the areas they lived in before imprisonment, living in the same environment and mixing with the same peers with whom they shared the habit.

Moving house and dumping all your old friends may be a little extreme, but the same principle holds. Make sure you've changed your patterns, destroyed those ingrained smoking rituals, thrown away all the smoking bits and pieces you have, and taken on a new identity as you, the non-smoker. Work with your partners or loved ones to continue supporting the new, improved you.

Celebrate your achievement. Blow next month's non-smoker's savings on a treat . Tell everyone you've stopped smoking, encourage others to join you (without boring them to death or telling them how easy it was for you). Share your insight about how to do it; offer to be their buddy while they stop.

Breathe deeply with satisfaction.

Q **I've read all the books on giving up and nothing appeals to me. What would you advise?**

A *Do you really want to give up? Of course you do, otherwise you wouldn't have bothered reading the books in the first place. Go back and ask yourself why you thought you wanted to give up. Then re-explore the options on offer and pick one. Give it a go. If you've tried and failed before, analyse why you didn't succeed. Try again or choose a different direction to head off in, but don't give it up. You can do it.*

Q **I've tried everything everyone's ever suggested already and nothing has worked. I'm wasting my time, aren't I?**

A *What, all of them? Try again. If nothing really grabs you, list all the ways you've tried, number them and pick a number at random. Then try it once more. Sometimes it's a question of choosing the right method for the right moment. Keep going until something kindles your interest. Never give up hope. You can be a non-smoker, too.*

Q **Some of ideas you've suggested sound really interesting but I don't have much money or the support network that you seem to think is so important. What should I do?**

A *Don't despair. If you look carefully there are some choices that cost nothing at all, and anyway if you're determined enough you can do it on your own. Lots of people have.*

How did it go?

The end...

Or is it a new beginning?

When this book went to print Peter had still not summoned up the enthusiasm to smoke his first cigarette. Clive has smoked his last, he hopes. But just in case of a relapse, he's keeping this book handy for emergencies. We hope that you are finding it useful too. Perhaps you've already calculated the costs (physical and financial), redecorated your home or joined forces with a group of others who want to quit. You're well on your way to a happier, healthier and smoke-free you.

So why not let us know all about it? Tell us how you got on. What did it for you? what really helped you smoke your last? Maybe you've got some tips of your own you want to share (see next page if so). And if you liked this book you may find we have even more brilliant ideas that could change other areas of your life for the better.

You'll find the Infinite Ideas crew waiting for you online at www.infideas.com

Or if you prefer to write, then send your letters to:
Stop smoking
The Infinite Ideas Company Ltd
36 St Giles, Oxford OX1 3LD, United Kingdom

We want to know what you think, because we're all working on making our lives better too. Give us your feedback and you could win a copy of another 52 *Brilliant Ideas* book of your choice. Or maybe get a crack at writing your own.

Good luck. Be brilliant.

Offer one

CASH IN YOUR IDEAS

We hope you enjoy this book. We hope it inspires, amuses, educates and entertains you. But we don't assume that you're a novice, or that this is the first book that you've bought on the subject. You've got ideas of your own. Maybe our author has missed an idea that you use successfully. If so, why not send it to yourauthormissedatrick@infideas.com, and if we like it we'll post it on our bulletin board. Better still, if your idea makes it into print we'll send you four books of your choice or the cash equivalent. You'll be fully credited so that everyone knows you've had another Brilliant Idea.

Offer two

HOW COULD YOU REFUSE?

Amazing discounts on bulk quantities of Infinite Ideas books are available to corporations, professional associations and other organizations.

For details call us on:
+44 (0)1865 514888
Fax: +44 (0)1865 514777
or e-mail: info@infideas.com

235

Where it's at...

Even more brilliant ideas...

Secrets of wine

Giles Kime

"Forget the wine snobbery, the 'bouquet reminiscent of elderberries drying on a nun's bicycle seat' approach; this pretentious imagery seems to dominate the world of wine and the wine bores who spout such expressions all have one thing in common. Their heads are full of other people's ideas. In Secrets of wine I offer an insider's guide to the real world of wine... the kind of advice that allows you to come up with your own thoughts. It's time for you to become a free-thinking drinker!"
Giles Kime

Available from all good bookshops or call us on + 44 (0) 1865 514888

Live longer

Sally Brown

"You can live a long and healthy life. Amazingly, anti-ageing scientists believe that only 1 in 10,000 people die of old age. The vast majority of us die prematurely from what we've come to call 'natural causes'. In fact, cell structure studies show that biologically our true lifespan is between 110 and 120 years!

All the advice you'll find in Live longer is achievable and can be fun too! Some of the best anti-ageing strategies involve having sex, drinking red wine and spending time with friends. So, live long and enjoy!" **– Sally Brown**